Studying Poetry
The Secret Gems of Poetry Revealed

Studymates

25 Key Topics in Business Studies
25 Key Topics in Human Resources
25 Key Topics in Marketing
Accident & Emergency Nursing
Business Organisation
Cultural Studies
English Legal System
European Reformation
Genetics
Hitler & Nazi Germany
Land Law
Organic Chemistry
Practical Drama & Theatre Arts
Revolutionary Conflicts
Social Anthropology
Social Statistics
Speaking Better French
Speaking English
Studying Chaucer
Studying History
Studying Literature
Understanding Maths

Many other titles in preparation

Studying Poetry

The Secret Gems of Poetry Revealed

Second edition

Richard Cochrane
BA(Hons) PhD

www.**studymates**.co.uk

Telephone: (01823) 432002
Fax: (01823) 430097
Website: http://www.studymates.co.uk

Note: The contents of this book are offered for the purposes of general guidance
only and no liability can be accepted for any loss or expense incurred as a result
of relying in particular circumstances on statements made in this book. Readers
are advised to check the current position with the appropriate authorities before
entering into personal arrangements.

Typeset by Kestrel Data, Exeter, Devon.
Printed in the UK by The Baskerville Press Ltd, Salisbury - www.baskervillepress.com

Contents

Preface

Studying poetry is an odd activity. Like most academic disciplines, it is plagued by jargon and complex terminology. The questions of what to do, as a student of poetry, and why to do it, can often be equally perplexing. Students of English Literature, either at A-level or during the first year of a degree, often find that there is a steep learning curve compared with the ways in which they have worked on poetry before.

This book aims to offer a framework for literary criticism as it is applied to poetry. It isn't a contribution to literary scholarship, and my readers' tutors will find many generalisations and simplifications herein. I make no apology for them. This is a book which, if you continue to study poetry, you will outgrow, but it provides a firm foundation from which to progress, whether you later move into modern literary theory or more traditional forms of criticism.

You will also find help here on essay writing, exam technique and other practical issues. This is not offered cynically, but in the knowledge that good students can easily be disadvantaged by making simple and correctable mistakes.

I would like to extend my personal gratitude to Clare Churly, not only for her editorial expertise and proofreading skills, but also for her long-suffering support and encouragement. I remain indebted to the staff of the English Literature department at Cardiff University, and especially to Dr John Peck who had the thankless task of driving me up the learning curve during my first year of study there.

Richard Cochrane
richardcochrane@studymates.co.uk

What is poetry?

One-minute summary – There are no cut and dried definitions of poetry, but its main feature – in contrast to prose – is its emphasis on form. Poetic form is a kind of structure into which the words of the poem are set. This analogy isn't perfect, but it is more useful than you might first imagine. Important examples of formal elements are metre, rhyme and visual structure. Features like these work together to produce the situation in which 'form enacts content'. This means that the form is just as important as the content in determining the meaning of the poem, and the relationship between the two is a key point for analysis. We end by looking at some important general skills which will help you to develop as a literary critic. In this chapter you will learn:

▶ what poetic form is
▶ how poetry and prose are related
▶ how to approach poetry
▶ the basic skills you need to produce good work
▶ some common mistakes

What poetic form is

What poetry isn't
Poetry isn't prose. That might sound obvious, but then you might ask, why? What *is* the difference between a poem and a piece of prose? What is it that makes a poem a poem?

Functional prose
Let's be unsophisticated for a moment. Let's say that a piece of 'straight' prose is a piece of writing which is designed to convey some meaning or other. Take this, for example:

'No left turn ahead'

This sentence says that you can't turn left at the next junction. You can say it in all sorts of other ways:

'Do not turn left at the next junction'
'Turning left is not permitted'
'Turn right or go straight on'

and so on. The differences are not terribly important. Some versions may be clearer than others, but that's the only real reason for choosing one over another. With functional prose, all you want is the information it contains: any version which gives you the right gist will do.

Literary prose

As we all know, prose is not only used for giving simple instructions and information. It can also be used to create literature. In that case, the choice of words is of great importance. There is more emphasis on the words themselves, and we are much less willing to change them without good reason. Poetry is like this too, but there is one important difference: poems emphasise *form* much more.

Don't expect a clear-cut explanation of the difference between poetry and prose. Just as you can have days when it isn't exactly hot or cold, so there are texts which are somewhere between poetry and literary prose. In practice, though, this situation turns out to be extremely unusual.

Turning a poem into prose

One way to make this difference clear is to try turning a poem into a piece of prose. Take, for example, 'The Shepherd' by William Blake:

How sweet is the shepherd's sweet lot!
From the morn to the evening he strays;
He shall follow his sheep all the day,
And his tongue shall be filled with praise.

For he hears the lamb's innocent call,
And he hears the ewe's tender reply;
He is watchful while they are in peace,
For they know when their Shepherd is nigh.

This seems pretty simple and direct – it certainly isn't fancy or complicated writing. That simplicity is part of what the poem is about, and straight off it's one of the things which is most likely to strike you about it.

If it were a piece of prose, it might look like this:

How sweet is the shepherd's sweet lot! From the morn to the evening he strays; he shall follow his sheep all the day, and his tongue shall be filled with praise. For he hears the lamb's innocent call, and he hears the ewe's tender reply; he is watchful while they are in peace, for they know when their Shepherd is nigh.

Suddenly it reads very strangely. Prose very rarely uses so many rhymes. The regular rhythm of the words sound odd, too, because prose tends to have a looser, more flexible rhythm which is closer to everyday speech.

This piece of text is not simple and direct any more; it's a complicated, rather peculiar piece of prose. When something is unusual, we tend to sit up and take notice of it – and that's likely to affect our experience of reading the text.

Form and content

Form and content both depend on the words in the text, and you can change either one by changing the words. Take, for example:

The cat sat on the mat

You can change the content, like this:

The cat sat near the mat

This changes the meaning of the text because you have changed the meaning of a word. You can also change the form:

The pussy sat on the rug

Now the text has lost its three little rhyming words. As a result, its form has been altered, although the sentence still says roughly the same thing. Believe it or not, if it were a poem this might also affect the meaning of the whole text.

Don't panic

The difference between form and content probably still looks pretty confusing. Don't panic! We are going to see a lot more examples of poetic form throughout this book. It might not become familiar in the next five minutes, but it won't take long to get used to how the concept works.

What poetic form is

Poetic form is a bit like a jelly mould. You can pour any flavour of jelly into the mould – you can even use blancmange – and the effect will be the same.

That is, the *form* will be the same. If you like jelly but hate blancmange, the chances are you'll realise that form isn't everything. In fact, when it comes to food, most of us think content is much more important than form: in poetry, on the contrary, form is extremely important.

In a poem, the mould might be very complicated or very simple, but it will give some structure to the text which prose usually lacks. When you analyse poetry, you'll need to pay at least as much attention to the mould as you do to the jelly.

The difference between poems and jellies

Cards on the table time, now. Our neat little analogy doesn't quite work. The fact is that the concept of a strict, clear-cut distinction between form and content is a bit spurious. So why bother with it? Well, there are at least four good reasons not to throw it away. They are:

1. It's useful. You'll find that you can make very sophisticated analyses using the form/content approach.

2. It's part of the history of poetry. A lot of poems use it in ways that you are likely to miss if you aren't looking for it.

3. It's also a part of the history of literary criticism. Most critics will assume you are familiar with it, so you need to understand it before you can understand their work.

4. There are plenty of whole books on the subject of form and content. We shouldn't be too keen to dismiss such a complex issue out of hand.

You will also find that, if and when you want to go beyond what's in this book, this knowledge will stand you in good stead.

Some major elements of form

In this section, we'll look at the main elements of a poem which can provide a formal structure. They're not the only formal elements, but they'll give you a broad picture of what poetic form is and how it works.

Metre

You'll remember the poem we looked at near the start of this chapter? One of its most prominent features was its regular rhythm. Prose doesn't normally have a rhythm like this. That doesn't mean it has no rhythm, just that its rhythms are irregular and flexible.

Rhythm is always important in poetry, but in many poems (particularly the sort written before this century) you'll find something more than just rhythm: you'll find metre.

▶ *Key point* – Metre is a regular rhythmic structure.

You'll learn the details of metre – and how to analyse it – in the next two chapters, but let's just take a brief look at this stanza from Shakespeare's 'The Phoenix and the Turtle'. A **stanza** is what most people call a 'verse' of a poem, a section separated from the rest by blank lines.

> Here the anthem doth commence:
> Love and constancy is dead,
> Phoenix and the turtle fled
> In a mutual flame from hence.

Read it aloud with an exaggerated rhythm, so you can hear the metre even if you can't analyse it yet. Now read this stanza aloud:

> Property was thus appalled,
> That the self was not the same;
> Single nature's double name
> Neither two nor one was called.

It's from the same poem, and I hope you can hear that they have exactly the same rhythm even though the words are completely different. This is our first example of poetic form, and it seems to fit the 'jelly mould' analogy rather well. The structure is the same in each case, even though the words which have been poured into it are different.

In the next chapter you'll find out how to take the words away and examine the form itself: the equivalent of removing the jelly so you can get a better look at the mould.

Homophony

You might think 'homophony' sounds like just the kind of obscure, technical terminology designed specifically to confuse you. You'd be wrong. 'Homo-' means 'the same' and '-phony' means 'sound', so 'homophony' just means 'the same sound'.

There are a lot of different kinds of homophony in poetry, and the gory details are all in chapter 4. The most common and best-known kind is **rhyme**. Look at the two stanzas which we saw in the last section. In each case, the first and last lines end with words which end in the same sound. This is another formal structure, and you'll soon learn how to separate it from the words of the poem.

Visual structure

This section is called 'visual structure' because it seems the best way to refer to 'how the text appears on the page'. In most prose – even the literary kind – this isn't a consideration. The text appears as a continuous block of words. In poetry, though, the words are laid out in lines and this often affects the meaning.

Although we don't analyse visual structure directly, we always need to be aware of the effect it has on the poem. Imagine if the first of the two stanzas we have just been looking at was written out like this instead:

Here the anthem
Doth commence: love
And constancy is dead, Phoenix
And the turtle fled in a mutual flame
from hence.

Perhaps you can't say why this is different, or exactly what effect it has, but I'm sure you will agree that the poem has changed. If you are not convinced, imagine you were an editor publishing a book of poems: would it be okay to set the text out on the page like this?

Form enacting content

'Form enacting content' is the theme of this whole book. It is an idea which you will learn gradually, by seeing it happen in different situations.

Look again at the first poem in this chapter – the one we turned into prose. At the time, we noticed that it has a simple, plain feel to both the rhythm and the system of rhymes. What might strike you is that the poem is actually about simplicity and innocence. This is exactly what 'form enacting content' is about: it's as if the form was acting out, or imitating, the subject of the poem.

Things won't always be so straightforward. Imagine if the poem had had very complex formal elements. It might leave you scratching your head over what looks like a contradiction. Contradictions are gold dust, however, and you will soon learn to greet them with open arms. The crucial thing to remember is that form and content will always be closely related, simply because the form and the content are two aspects of the same poem.

Key poetry study skills

We will keep on spotting useful techniques and skills that you will want to develop as you sharpen your ability to make sense of poetry. There are some tips and skills, though, which are absolutely essential. Without them, you are likely to make some very basic mistakes. These skills are:

▶ close reading
▶ using evidence
▶ building an argument
▶ looking for complexity
▶ avoiding value judgements
▶ analysing the poem, not the poet
▶ using good, modern editions
▶ reading around

Close reading

'Close reading' means scrutinising every detail of a text. This is particularly important for poetry. Often, poems are extremely short; you won't get anything out of them if you give them the attention you would pay to a paragraph in an airport novel.

Poems are crammed with detail. Examine every word.

Squeeze every drop of meaning from the text. In a novel, you're unlikely to miss anything crucial if you don't do this; in poetry, you will.

When you analyse a poem, your level of inquiry can get to the point where you're asking questions about the nature of language itself. That's how fundamental your reading can get. Pursue it to the very limit. If this seems impossible now, fear not. You'll find plenty of approaches to help you with it throughout this book.

Using evidence

One mistake that most students make at the start of their careers is to say what they *think* or *feel* about a poem without giving evidence. I call this the 'Pub Bore' tendency. The Pub Bore goes on at great length about his/her opinions without supplying the facts to back them up. You can't argue with the Pub Bore, who prefers unfounded opinions to evidence and rational argument. As a result, the audience quietly and politely slips away. As a literary critic, you need to approach your work in a more professional way than this.

▶ *Key study tip* – If you have something to say about a poem, provide evidence which shows that you're saying something reasonable, even something enlightening.

Don't worry: we all started out as Pub Bores. That's how literature tends to get taught at school, and it may well have helped you to get interested in the subject – you might even have developed some pretty strong instincts in the process. Without those instincts, you'll find it hard to become a really fine critic, but on their own they won't raise your work above GCSE level. Fortunately, this book is all about how to provide evidence to back up your arguments.

Building an argument

The opposite of the Pub Bore is the Anorak. The Anorak rejoices in lists of dry, boring facts, tables of information and complicated charts. The Anorak has forgotten that it's important to make sense of what the poem *means*, not just what it's made of.

Just remember that a poem isn't a puzzle; it's a work of art. Understanding a poem is more than just mapping out metrical structures and rhyme schemes. That means that your evidence should develop into an argument about what the poem is about, rather than being scattered here and there without any coherent thread. You'll find a detailed explanation of how to do this in chapter 9.

Looking for complexity

In part, the purpose of an essay about a poem is simply to show that the poem is interesting, that there's more to it than meets the eye. It's your job to help people to understand why a poem might be fascinating and complex, even if it looks straightforward at first glance. Of course, some poems will make you work harder than others on this.

So, avoid the temptation to reduce the poem to a complete understanding so that no-one need ever read it again. Incoherence, contradictions, inconsistencies and other obstacles are your friends, not your enemies. They are vital tools which will help you develop your essay into something much more interesting and sophisticated. You'll see how as we work through this book.

Avoiding value judgements

Having said this, your intention is not to say, 'this is a great poem'. Complexity doesn't always mean greatness, otherwise we would all be getting excited about local government bureaucracy. Even if you don't like a poem, there will still be plenty of interesting things you can say about it.

The bottom line is that we're dealing with works of literature here, and your preferences may not be shared by the people reading (and marking) your work:

You . . .	Your reader . . .	Your reader says . . .
Liked the poem	Likes the poem	Big deal
Liked the poem	Doesn't like the poem	Bad call
Didn't like the poem	Likes the poem	Wrong again . . .
Didn't like the poem	Doesn't like the poem	So what?

Figure 1-1

This is a no-win scenario for you: avoid it like bad medicine.

Analysing the poem, not the poet

As a poetry student, you're not a psychologist, and you're not a biographer. Don't try to use the poem to work out what the poet was thinking or feeling. It's better not to speculate on what the poet intended or wanted to say, because you'll never really know. Stick to the text of the poem and you won't go far wrong.

When a critic talks about what the *poet* means, instead of what the *poem* means, we say they're using the 'intentional fallacy': assuming that because a poem says something, the poet must have thought it. Knowing a bit about when a poem was written and the style it's written in will often help you, but trying to delve into the author's psychology will lead you up a blind alley.

Because of this, critics often use the term 'narrator' instead of 'poet'. The narrator is an imaginary character who speaks the words of the poem; you can say what you like about the narrator, as long as it's supported by the words of the poem, without ever mentioning the poet at all.

Using good, modern editions

'Bargain' editions of poems might look tempting, but check to see what you are getting. A full-price edition will probably have a foreword written by an expert and, more importantly, footnotes.

Why are footnotes important? Well, poems often contain unusual, old-fashioned or just plain obscure words. Unless someone tells you what they mean, you will be left guessing, as in this stanza from Robert Browning's 'Soliloquy of the Spanish Cloister':

> Blasted lay that rose-acacia
>   We're so proud of! *Hy, Zy, Hine!* . . .
> 'St, there's vespers! *Plena gratiâ*
>   *Ave, Virgo!* . . . Gr-r-r – you swine!

So, you bought a budget edition of Browning's *Selected Poems,* did you? Bad luck! My edition tells me exactly what all these obscurities are about – in footnotes.

Reading around

One last piece of advice before we get started. Poems usually refer to all sorts of other things outside themselves. If you know about the thing the poem's referring to, you'll understand it; if not, you might miss the whole point. That's just life – nobody knows everything – but you can be smart and try to cut down a little on the number of times it happens.

▶ *Key study tip* – Read introductory books on history, theology, philosophy, painting, music – anything which might be relevant. Don't get bogged down in detail; give yourself a broad, basic education. Knowledge like this is impossible to fake, and if you demonstrate it you're likely to impress your readers.

Tutorial

Progress questions

1. How does reading poetry differ from reading prose?

2. List three important elements of poetic form.

3. What is meant by the phrase, 'form enacting content'?

4. List the eight basic skills which you will need to take with you throughout your career as a literary critic.

Discussion points
In most of the discussion points in this book, you will find using a poem to focus the discussion very useful.

1. Is form really distinct from content?

2. Why does it matter what poems mean? Why is it worthwhile to study them?

Practical assignments
1. Take a line from a poem, and try changing one or more words so as to alter:

   (a) just the content
   (b) just the form
   (c) both
   (d) neither

Not as easy as it sounds, is it? That's because form and content are so closely related in a piece of poetry.

2. Pick a short poem from an anthology and examine the language as closely as possible. See how much you can spot which you missed on first reading.

3. If you have studied poetry before, dig out your old essays. See if you can identify:

   (a) where you were talking about formal elements (probably not too often)

(b) where you were focussed on content (probably most of the time)

Study tip

1. As you work your way through this book, you might like to use one or two poems as 'benchmarks'. When you come across a new concept, see if it applies to one of your benchmark poems: it might not, but if it does it can be rather enlightening.

2. This book contains a lot of technical terminology. Above all, these words are there to help you to remember particular features of a poem which might be significant. Learning them all by heart on a first reading isn't recommended – instead, aim to develop the analytical skill which they relate to. There's a glossary at the back of this book defining all of the technical terms used in this book.

2

Regular Metre

One-minute summary – Metre is the rhythmic element of poetry, which is one aspect of poetic form. In the first chapter, we talked about poetic form as a sort of mould into which the words are fitted: a rhythmic structure is one sort of mould which poets use to give form to their writing. Here we'll be looking at regular metres; in the next chapter, we'll see how poets use irregularity to create variety and effect subtle changes in meaning. Just as most music has a strong, regular beat, so does most poetry. Many of the best-known poems – particularly older ones – are actually 'lyrics' which were originally sung to music. Because metre is musical, remember to use your ears as well as your eyes; it will even help if you read the examples in this chapter aloud. In this chapter, you will learn:

▶ what metres are made up of: syllables, stress and feet (believe it or not)
▶ how to analyse a metrical structure

What is metre?

OK, this is the boring part. Let's be honest, regular metre is nothing to get excited about. The good stuff comes when we look at irregularities in the next chapter, but you'll never understand an irregularity unless you can see what the regular structure surrounding it is.

These are the bits that metre is made up of:

1. Syllables are composed of a vowel, usually accompanied by one or two consonant sounds.

2. A metrical 'foot' is composed of a number of syllables.

3. A sequence of 'feet' makes up a metre.

4. The metre is the overall rhythmic structure of the poem.

This section explains what each of these terms means and how they fit together.

What is a syllable?

Vowels

There are far more vowel *sounds* than the five *letters* a, e, i, o and u. Roughly speaking, a vowel is a sound which you can make by breathing through your vocal chords and out of your mouth. Try saying 'ah', 'ooh', 'oh', 'eee', 'air' and 'or' for some examples – make them long sounds to get a feel for how different these are from, say, 'p' or 'g' (the sounds, not the names of the letters, which end in vowel sounds: 'pee' and 'gee').

Consonants

A consonant, basically, is any letter which isn't a vowel. Again, remember that we are not just talking about individual letters like d, m, g, f and p. English contains a lot of what linguists call 'consonantal clusters' like 'str' (as in 'strong'). Each of these, too, is a consonant sound.

A	Vowel only
Me	Consonant + vowel
On	Vowel + consonant
Cat	Consonant + vowel + consonant
Ship	As above ('sh' is a consonantal cluster)
Gnome	As above (the first and last letters are not pronounced)

Figure 2-1

Syllables
A syllable is a single beat in the rhythm of speech. Each beat contains a vowel sound and, usually, one or two consonant sounds as well. So, these are all syllables:

Polysyllabic words
We have just seen a list of 'monosyllabic' words – words with only one syllable. Most English words, though, are 'polysyllabic': they are made of several syllables arranged together.

'London', for example, has two syllables. Say the name slowly and deliberately: Lon-don. You should clearly hear two beats, two distinct parts to the word which make a rhythmic pattern: Lon-don. 'Manchester' has three syllables: Man-ches-ter. 'Nottinghamshire' has four: No-tting-ham-shire. If you'd like to see more examples like this, look in a dictionary. Most dictionaries give a pronunciation with each word which shows its different syllables.

Words with more than four syllables are unusual in English. Although many do exist, they tend to be obscure or technical terms, like pol-y-syl-ab-ic. The vast majority of English words have one, two or three syllables.

Exceptions
There are some syllables that do not have conventional vowel sounds. Think of 'bubble' – definitely a two-syllable word, bu-bble. Yet the second syllable has no vowel sound in it. Other examples are 'spasm' (spa-sm) and 'riddle' (ri-ddle).

The sounds 'lll', 'rrr' and 'zzz' are a lot like vowels, and in a few words – not many – they act as vowels to form a separate syllable. So don't be surprised if you hear two beats but only see one vowel sound: your ears may be right after all.

What is stress?
Syllables, much like people, can be either stressed or unstressed. A stressed syllable is emphasised more than an unstressed one. Understanding stress is absolutely essential to being able to analyse metre.

Here are the conventional marks for stress in metrical analysis:

/ stressed syllable

⌣ unstressed syllable

Spotting the difference between unstressed and stressed syllables gets easier with practice; the rest of this section will help you develop the knack.

Stress in polysyllabic words
Here are some polysyllabic words, with the stressed and unstressed syllables marked. Say the words clearly and slowly to yourself – the secret is to exaggerate the way you say them, and that way their rhythmic patterns will be all the more obvious:

/ ⌣   ⌣
Pho-to-graph

⌣ / ⌣   ⌣
Pho-to-graph-y

/ ⌣ / ⌣
Pho-to-graph-ic

If you want more examples, pick up the dictionary again; as well as breaking words into syllables, they usually show which syllable should be stressed. Some general rules are:

1. A stress never follows another stress.
2. Finding more than two unstressed syllables in a row is very rare.
3. Words often start with a stressed syllable.

Stress in monosyllabic words
Monosyllabic words can be either stressed or unstressed, depending on their place in the sentence. The general rules for this are similar to those for polysyllabic words, but vaguer:

1. Two stresses are quite rarely found together.
2. More than two unstressed words together is also unusual.
3. More important words are often stressed; words like 'a' and 'the' are usually unstressed.

So, let's take a simple sentence containing only monosyllables: 'I am a mole and I live in a hole'. Say it (go ahead: no-one's listening) and hear the rhythm of the words:

/ ⌣ ⌣ / ⌣ ⌣ / ⌣ ⌣ /
I am a mole and I live in a hole

You might like to imagine that the stressed words are written in *italics*, for added emphasis:

I am a *mole* and I *live* in a *hole*

Try stressing different words and you'll see that it feels much more natural to say the sentence as it's written above.

Don't panic
Identifying stressed and unstressed syllables will get easier when you have a complete theory of metre, which you will by the end of this chapter.

   In the meantime, here's a trick to help you check your analyses. Try using 'dum' for stressed and 'da' for unstressed syllables. It emphasises the musical element nicely. 'I am a mole and I live in a hole' would go '*dum* da da *dum* da da *dum* da da *dum*'. Just don't let anyone hear you doing it.

What are feet?
Analysis without feet
Armed with what you've already learned, you can go ahead and analyse rhythmic structures to your heart's content. The problem is, all you'll get is a bunch of '/'s and '⌣'s. Let's analyse the first of the stanzas from 'The Turtle and the Phoenix' which we saw in Chapter 1:

Here the anthem doth commence:	/ ˘ / ˘ / ˘ /
Love and constancy is dead,	/ ˘ / ˘ / ˘ /
Phoenix and the turtle fled	/ ˘ / ˘ / ˘ /
In a mutual flame from hence.	/ ˘ / ˘ / ˘ /

The regular rhythm which we noticed when we first read it is obvious from the patterns of stressed and unstressed syllables: each line goes '/ ˘ / ˘ / ˘ /' (dum da dum da dum da dum, if you prefer), but that doesn't really tell us much about the poem.

What we need to do is break this down into 'feet'. A foot is a unit of two or three syllables – usually a mixture of stressed and unstressed – which is repeated to make a regular rhythm. There are four basic kinds.

Iamb

Pronounced 'eye-am', this foot has one unstressed syllable followed by one stressed syllable, as in this line from Andrew Marvell's 'The Fair Singer':

˘ /	˘ /	˘ /	˘ /	˘ /
I could	have fled	from one	but sing-	-ly fair

Figure 2-2

Try saying the line repeatedly to get a feel for the rhythm.

Trochee

Pronounced 'troe-key', it has one stressed syllable followed by an unstressed syllable – like a reversed iamb. Here's an example from Henry David Thoreau's 'Low-Anchored Cloud':

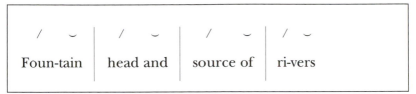

Figure 2-3

Anapest

The anapest (pronounced 'an-a-pest') has three syllables: two unstressed and then one stressed. It's much less common than the trochee or iamb. Here is an example from Lord Byron's 'The Destruction of Sennacherib':

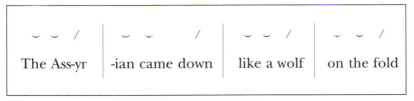

Figure 2-4

Repeat the line over and over and you will soon hear the three-beat rhythm of this foot.

Dactyl

Pronounced 'dak-till', this is another three-syllable foot. It is exactly the opposite of an anapest, as in this line from Thomas Hardy's 'The Voice':

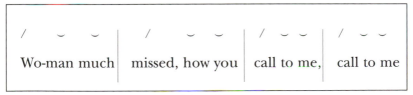

Figure 2-5

The three-syllable feet are much less common than the iamb and trochee.

Number of feet per line

The number of feet in a line is indicated by the following words:

monometer	one foot	(very rare)
bimeter	two feet	(very rare)
trimeter	three feet	(quite unusual)
quatrameter	four feet	(very common)
pentameter	five feet	(very common)
hexameter	six feet	(quite common)
heptameter	seven feet	(quite unusual)
octameter	eight feet	(unusual)
nonameter	nine feet	(quite rare)
decameter	ten feet	(very rare)

So 'iambic pentameter' (the most common metre of all) has five iambs in each line. You needn't memorise all of these technical terms straight away. Understanding the general concept – that poetic metre is a rhythm made up of repeated units – is much more important.

Variations on the classical feet

Trailing syllables

Trailing syllables come at the end of a line, and are not part of a foot. They are sometimes referred to as 'extra-metrical' or 'hypermetrical'. In 'The Phoenix and the Turtle', Shakespeare has added a trailing stress to the end of each line:

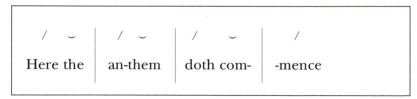

Figure 2-5a

This may have been designed to give each line a firm ending – what used to be called a 'masculine' ending.

He does the opposite in Hamlet's famous speech, the first line
of which goes like this:

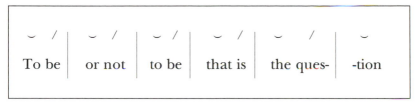

Figure 2-6

Here, the iambic feet (‿ /) are finished off by an unstressed
syllable; this was once called a 'feminine' ending. In
Shakespeare's time, this was thought to be weaker and more
uncertain than the masculine ending (in which the line
finishes with a stress).

▶ *Note* – You might not be completely convinced by this
   version of the stresses in Hamlet's line. Neither am I. You
   will see a more sophisticated version in the next chapter.

Although the term comes from French grammar, the
traditional idea that women are weak and uncertain, and men
are rational and strong, is definitely implied when someone
uses the term 'feminine' or 'masculine' ending.

Leading syllables
A leading syllable comes at the start of a line, and like the
trailing version it is not part of a metrical foot. They are almost

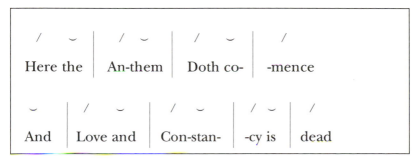

Figure 2-7

always unstressed; that's just the way that metre tends to work. A classic example of a leading syllable is an 'and' placed at the start of a line. Imagine if Shakespeare had written as in fig 2-7. Because of the regularity of the surrounding poem, we can easily think of the 'and' on line two as an addition which is not part of the regular metrical structure of the line as a whole.

Because leading syllables tend to be unstressed, this is not such a good analysis of Shakespeare's metre:

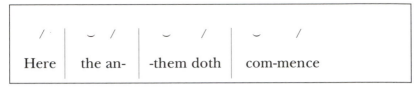

Figure 2-8

The first syllable just sounds too important to be an added extra. If the surrounding lines were all in trochees without leading syllables, then it might make more sense, but as a regular feature it's not too convincing.

▶ *Note* – Actually, leading and trailing syllables are often examples of irregularities, but sometimes they're used regularly throughout a poem, as in 'The Phoenix and the Turtle'.

Elision

'Elision' means compressing two syllables into one by missing out (eliding) one of the vowel sounds. Everyday examples include 'can't', 'it's' and 'I'm'. Common poetic ones include 't'was' (it was) and the contraction of 'the' to 'th'', as in 'th' inn', which makes 'the inn' (two syllables) into a one-syllable unit.

More subtle effects of elision come when a regular metre encourages the reader to elide a sound even when there is no indication (like an apostrophe). Take the example we saw above, the first line of 'The Destruction of Sennacherib':

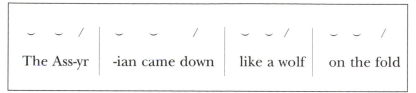

Figure 2-9

Here, the word 'Assyrian' is scanned as ⌣ / ⌣ ('A-ssyr-ian'), but say the word on its own and you're much more likely to say A-ssyr-i-an – four syllables, ⌣ / ⌣ ⌣. Read the whole line with this pronunciation, though, and it sounds quite wrong. The overall rhythm encourages the reader to squeeze the two vowel sounds together to form a single syllable.

Don't panic
Metrical analysis is full of technical terms. Don't be put off by them. No one is going to be overly impressed just because you can say 'anapaestic hexameter' anyway. What *will* impress is your ability to use this information to understand the poem – something we will come to shortly.

Summary of terms
Here is a quick run-down of the terms defined in this section:

1. Foot – a collection of two or three syllables, usually one stressed and the others unstressed.

2. The common feet are trochee, iamb, dactyl and anapest.

3. Trailing syllable – a syllable at the end of a line, which isn't part of a metrical foot.

4. Leading syllable – a syllable at the start of a line, which isn't part of a metrical foot.

5. Masculine ending – a line which ends with a stressed

syllable – traditionally a 'strong' ending which suggests completion.

6. Feminine ending – a line which ends with an unstressed syllable – traditionally a weaker, more uncertain resolution.

7. Elision – missing out a vowel sound to create the desired rhythmic effect.

Metre itself

The metre of a poem is its overall, general rhythmic structure. 'The Phoenix and the Turtle' has a very simple metre: trochaic trimeter with a trailing stress, if you want to be technical:

$$| \, / \, \smile \, | \, / \, \smile \, | \, / \, \smile \, | \, / \, |$$

if you want to write it out that way, or 'dum da dum da dum da dum' if you're lecturing the local nursery school (always use the technical version in essays).

Other poems often have more complex metres. This is a slightly less simple one – an excerpt from Thomas Gray's 'Ode on the Death of a Favourite Cat':

'Twas on a lofty vase's side,	$\smile / \smile / \smile / \smile /$
Where China's gayest art had dyed	$\smile / \smile / \smile / \smile /$
The azure flowers that blow;	$\smile / \smile / \smile /$
Demurest of the tabby kind,	$\smile / \smile / \smile / \smile /$
The pensive Selima, reclined,	$\smile / \smile / \smile / \smile /$
Gazed on the lake below.	$\smile / \smile / \smile /$

Fairly obviously, the structure here is two lines of iambic quatrameter (four iambs, $\smile /$) followed by one line of iambic trimeter (just three feet). This pattern continues throughout the poem.

Notice that the structure actually tells you how to pronounce the cat's name. You might have been tempted to say 'Se-li-ma' , like 'Selina', but Gray implies that the proper stresses fall on the first and last syllables, '*Se*-li-*ma*', which makes her seem much more exotic since it's an unusual pattern for an English word.

▶ *Note* - You might not feel that my analysis of the last line is right, and I would agree with you. Read it aloud. It's passable, but the first two words feel awkward – 'Gazed *on* the *lake* be-*low*'. We'll see how to make a better version in the next chapter.

Regular metre in context

A potted history of metre

Whole books have been written on the history of metre in English poetry, and this isn't one of them. It's important to realise, though, that what's common in one century might be unusual in others, and that meanings change over time. The more poetry you read, the more you'll become aware of this.

Here is a very brief outline. It doesn't really scratch the surface of the subject, but it will give some basic pointers:

▶ *Around 1400–1700* – The Renaissance, and the introduction to England of 'syllabic metre'. Poems began to follow strict metrical patterns.

▶ *Around 1700–1850* – The Augustans and Romantics developed the use of looser overall structures – for example, iambic pentameter with the odd line of trimeter – but within each line the metre was still adhered to relatively closely.

▶ *Around 1850–1920* – Gradually, poets began experimenting with more and more irregular metrical systems until, with the rise of Modernism, some abandoned regular metres entirely. After 1920, poets went off in all sorts of directions, but it is fair to say that metrical poetry in the twentieth century always feels either popular and folksy (think of Pam Ayers) or old-fashioned (like A E Housman).

What a regular metre means

Syllabic metre was relatively new in the renaissance, so following its rules was a sign of sophistication. The arts in the Renaissance generally had a tendency towards formality; the word 'renaissance' means re-birth, referring to the re-discovery of ancient Greek art, science and philosophy. With that came creative work which valued formal relationships more than ever before in Europe.

By the time of the Romantics, regular metre had become rather *passé*. Sophistication came to be linked with a different kind of complexity: skilful variations on metrical structures. The Romantics tended to revere nature; think of the natural world's tendency to produce many variations on a single design.

'The Phoenix and the Turtle' is a serious poem, given a stately rhythm by those trailing stresses we spotted earlier. The regularity of the metre is a part of its rather intellectual, formal style. In Blake's Romantic poem about the shepherd, though, the rural innocence it describes is *enacted* by its formal simplicity. Both have regular metres, but the meanings of these metres are quite different.

Warning!
You can see that knowing when a poem was written is important here. Sometimes – as in some 'unseen' exams – you won't have that knowledge. In that case, don't risk any assumptions. The more poetry you read, the better you will get at recognising work from different periods, often by the words used and the subject-matter. If you're unsure, don't leap to any conclusions about regular metres: you may be well off the mark. You will still be able to use metrical irregularities in your analysis, though – we will see how in the next chapter.

Tutorial

Progress questions
1. What are the four most common metrical feet?

2. List the three broad historical periods in the history of English metrical poetry.

3. What are leading and trailing syllables?

4. What are masculine and feminine endings?

5. What's elision?

Points for discussion
Is there always one correct metrical analysis for any line of poetry? If not, how can you decide which one to use?

Practical assignments
1. Think of some nursery rhymes and work out their metrical structures. They tend to be very regular. You can do the same with many pop songs.

2. Try to find examples of verse containing leading and trailing syllables.

Study tips
1. Use a dictionary to check your analyses of polysyllabic words.

2. Practice is the key to getting the hang of metrical analysis. Work on it every day if you find it difficult, and it soon it will become second nature to you.

3

Metrical Irregularities

One-minute summary – If all poems went 'dum da dum da dum' and so on, the rhythmic side of poetry would be pretty boring. Fortunately, almost all poems use ingenious irregularities to vary the rhythm and make things more interesting. The irregularities also give the critic (that's you) a chance to find extra, subtle alterations in meaning in the poem. These are gold dust when it comes to writing essays. Always remember that *meaning* is what matters. If you can't explain how one of these formal elements affects the meaning of a poem, it's not worth mentioning it. Few examiners hand out marks for spotting spondees and enjambment if you can't say anything except 'Look! There's one!' It isn't train-spotting. Remember, too, that memorising all of these technical words isn't the point; the point is seeing an irregularity and saying what it *means,* not sticking a label on it and waiting for someone to offer a round of applause. In this chapter, you will learn:

▶ how to spot and understand irregularities in metrical poems
▶ how to handle free verse
▶ more about metre and meaning

Irregularities in metrical verse

Underlying metre
The concept of 'underlying metre' is a very useful one. When poets introduce irregularities in their metres, they aren't normally changing the structure itself, just making a variation on it.

Some poems have a very subtle underlying metre with many variations to give it an elastic, unpredictable movement.

The more irregularities there are, the more likely it is that the poem is from a later historical period, though this is a guideline rather than a rule.

Substitution of feet

Often, poets substitute one foot for another to give some variety. This can be quite surprising, drawing special attention to the word or words which cause the irregularity.

You might not, for instance, agree with my original ‘scanning’ of the last line of Gray’s stanza:

⌣ /	⌣ /	⌣ /
Gazed on	the lake	be-low

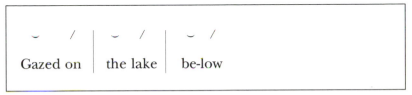

Figure 3-1

I wrote it that way to make the example clearer, but this is much better:

/ ⌣	⌣ /	⌣ /
Gazed on	the lake	be-low

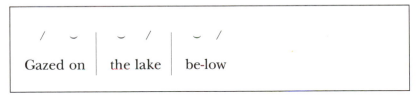

Figure 3-2

The first trochee has been replaced by an iamb: notice the very different rhythmic feel this gives the line: ‘Dum da-da Dum da Dum’ instead of ‘Da Dum Da Dum Da Dum’. You will see one of the effects this has in a moment.

▶ *Technical note* - When the stress pattern of a foot is reversed – for example turning ⌣ / into / ⌣ This is sometimes called ‘inversion’ or ‘reversion’.

Addition or removal of feet

Sometimes, variation of the metrical length of lines is part of the regular structure, as in the short lines in Gray's cat poem. Other times, you will find short lines interspersed just for variety, or for dramatic effect. It can be quite startling when a line unexpectedly comes to an abrupt stop.

Additional feet can feature in exactly the same way. Often a longer line is used to tie up an idea and give a sense of finality, as if the extra foot or two put a cap on the matter, as satirised here in Alexander Pope's 'Essay on Criticism':

> Then, at the last and only couplet fraught
> With some unmeaning thing they call a thought,
> A needless Alexandrine ends the song
> That, like a wounded snake, drags its slow length along.

Alexandrine is an old-fashioned name for a line of iambic hexameter – that is, one iamb more than the underlying metre. At other times, the effect will be quite different. Much depends on the content and the surrounding metrical structure.

The use of 'foreshortened' and 'elongated' lines as irregularities (not regular features) really began in the Augustan and Romantic periods. They are seldom found in earlier writing.

Caesura

A caesura is a pause or break in the metre. It is usually caused by two stresses coming side by side. 'The Phoenix and the Turtle' could be said to contain a caesura between each line, since each line starts and finishes with a stress. When you read the poem aloud, you might find each line feels quite separate from the others because of the pauses which the stresses force you to put between them; this is the main reason why its pace seems so slow and stately.

Usually, though, a caesura is an irregular feature. It makes the poem grind to a halt before it gets itself re-started again. Look at the last two lines of Gray's stanza:

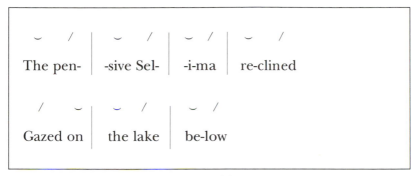

Figure 3-3

We know that the poem is about the death of the cat. The hesitation between the two stresses, followed by the unexpected rush of the two unstressed syllables, enact the precarious position of the cat – they are rather like the moving camera in an action sequence of a film.

Caesurae (that's the plural) are often made more effective by the use of long syllables like 'lined' and 'gazed'. Most syllables are short, punchy sounds. Longer ones tend to draw out and slow the rhythm anyway, which makes the caesura more effective.

Here is one last example. Many people would read Hamlet's famous line like this:

⏑ /	⏑ /	⏑ /	/ ⏑ ⏑	/ ⏑
To be	or not	to be	that is the	ques-tion

Figure 3-4

The underlying metre of *Hamlet* is iambic pentameter, and so the version we gave at first wasn't unreasonable, but this one is more accurate. By substituting a dactyl for the fourth iamb and a trochee for the fifth, Shakespeare manages to get a caesura at the comma as well as a feminine ending. You might say this enacts the stumbling uncertainty of the speech as a whole.

Spondees and pyrrhics

Spondees and pyrrhics are special kinds of metrical foot:

Spondee: / /
Pyrrhic: ⌣ ⌣

They are never used in regular metres, but sometimes appear as variations. When they do they often cause quite dramatic rhythmic changes. A rare example of a line wholly in spondees is Samuel Taylor Coleridge's 'Slow spondee stalks, strong foot' – though even here it would be more usual to read 'spondee' as / ⌣.

The spondee normally serves to slow the poem down, as in this line from G M Hopkins' 'God's Grandeur':

⌣ /	/ ⌣	⌣ /	/ /	⌣ /
Is bare	now, nor	can foot	feel, be-	-ing shod

Figure 3-5

The underlying metre is iambic pentameter (this is easier to work out when you can see the whole poem), but the second foot is a trochee and the fourth a spondee. This creates a situation in which the stresses crowd together.

Here, each word in the spondee takes on added weight by virtue of all those stressed syllables. A pyrrhic, on the other hand, usually speeds the line along as if cramming extra words into the metrical scheme, which tends to emphasise the next stressed syllable.

A spondee might or might not create a caesura; the line from Hopkins is so crammed with stresses that there doesn't seem to be a definite pause so much as a general slowing down.

A pyrrhic can produce a caesura, too. Compare Hamlet's line with Henry IV's famous war-cry:

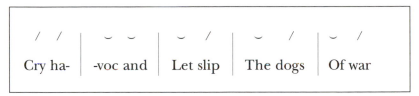

/ /	⌣ ⌣	⌣ /	⌣ /	⌣ /
Cry ha-	-voc and	Let slip	The dogs	Of war

Figure 3-6

Here the first iamb is replaced by a spondee, and the next becomes a pyrrhic, partly for variety and partly to give even more emphasis to the spondee. The result is that 99 per cent of actors like to shout the first two words, and then pause in the middle of the pyrrhic before continuing. The three unstressed syllables in a row are enough to create a caesura; its exact placing is determined by the way the words fit into the formal scheme.

Foregrounding

Effects like caesura and substituted feet often make the word(s) involved more noticeable than the surrounding text. Literary critics call this 'foregrounding'. The results can be very subtle: you will need to pay attention to the content as well as the form if you are to make much sense of them.

Free verse

Isn't free verse simply 'verse without any rhythm'? No, it isn't. All language has rhythmic elements. It's just that free verse doesn't have a regular, repetitive one.

Many poems that look like free verse actually do have metrical structures. Whenever you see a free verse poem, quickly jot down an analysis: you might be surprised. The most unlikely poems turn out to have perfectly regular – if rather weird – underlying metres.

Looking for metrical patterns

If there is no overall metrical form to the poem, perhaps there are little areas of metre - a few lines of iambic pentameter, for instance, tucked away amongst the rhythmic chaos. T S Eliot's 'The Waste Land' is a famous free verse poem, most of which is actually written in regular metres.

This can serve to set them apart from the rest of the writing; it can also remind the reader of more traditional writing. In 'The Waste Land', all kinds of different poetic styles are jumbled together to reflect the confused state of poetry at the time Eliot was writing.

Alternatively, you might find a loose metrical arrangement, as in 'Low-Anchored Cloud' by Henry David Thoreau:

Low-anchored cloud,	| / ⌣ ⌣ | /–
Newfoundland air,	| / ⌣ ⌣ | /–
Fountainhead and source	
of rivers,	|/ ⌣ | / ⌣ | / ⌣ | / ⌣ |
Dew-cloth, dream drapery,	|/ ⌣ | / / | ⌣ ⌣ |
And napkin spread by fays;	| ⌣ / | ⌣ / | ⌣ / |
Drifting meadow of the air	| / ⌣ | / ⌣ | / ⌣ | /–
Where bloom the daisied banks	
and violets,	–⌣ | / ⌣ | / ⌣ | / ⌣ | / ⌣ | ⌣–
And in whose fenny labyrinth	⌣ / | ⌣ / | ⌣ / | ⌣ /
The bittern booms and heron	
wades;	⌣ / | ⌣ / | ⌣ / | ⌣ /
Spirit of lakes and seas and rivers,	| / ⌣ ⌣ | / ⌣ | / ⌣ | / ⌣ |
Bear only perfumes and scent	–/ | / ⌣ | / ⌣ | ⌣ / |
Of healing herbs to just men's	
fields!	| ⌣ / | ⌣ / | ⌣ / | ⌣ / |

Metre helps give shape to this poem. It would be confusing and monotonous if it were all in one metre. Instead Thoreau does this:

2 anapaestic lines
2 trochaic lines

1 iambic line
1 trochaic line
an ambiguous line, which is closer to trochees than iambs
2 iambic lines
2 trochaic lines, the first starting with an anapaest
1 iambic line

This, at the very least, gives the poem some variety as a way to overcome its lack of action. The anapaests at the start even get a reprise, like an introduction from a song coming back before the end. You'd also notice, I'm sure, the regularity of metre within each line: a trochaic line typically only contains trochees, and so on (with the exception of line 4). Further, each line is in either trimeter or quatrameter. The regularity within each line contrasts with the irregularity of the poem as a whole.

What if there's no metrical form at all?

Even when there are no regular metrical features, you shouldn't forget about rhythm entirely. You can still talk about the use of spondees and pyrrhics to slow down or speed up the pace of a line, and you can still find caesurae and note which words they serve to emphasise. You can also look for short, staccato lines which have a quick, simple delivery, and contrast them with long, rhythmically varied lines whose content is likely to be quite different.

Tutorial

Progress questions

1. What are spondees and pyrrhics?

2. What is foregrounding?

3. Here is the second stanza of Matthew Arnold's 'Dover Beach'. Don't worry about what these lines mean: they're taken out of context and look pretty obscure on their own:

Sophocles long ago	l / ⌣ ⌣ l / ⌣ l /–
Heard it on the Aegean,	
and it brought	l / ⌣ l / ⌣ ⌣ l / ⌣ l / ⌣ l /–
Into his mind the turbid	
ebb and flow	l / ⌣ ⌣ l / ⌣ l / ⌣ l / ⌣ l /–
Of human misery; we	l ⌣ / l ⌣ / l ⌣ / l /–
Find also in the sound a	
thought,	l ⌣ / l ⌣ / l ⌣ / l ⌣ / l
Hearing it by this distant	
northern sea.	l / ⌣ ⌣ l / ⌣ l / ⌣ l / ⌣ l /–

Try to make sense of this irregular metre – or is it actually free verse?

4. Finally, here is Alexander Pope having a laugh at the expense of poets who over-use these tricks, but illustrating them rather well:

> When Ajax strives some rock's vast weight to throw,
> The line too labors, and the words move slow;
> Not so when swift Camilla scours the plain,
> Flies o'er the unbending corn, and skims along the main

Make your own metrical analysis of these lines, with comments.

Points for discussion
1. Should all poetry be metrical, or is free verse a more 'natural' form of expression?

2. If you take away metre and rhyme, doesn't a poem just turn into a piece of prose written out in a funny way?

Practical assignments
1. Compare and contrast the metrical structures of short poems by Shakespeare, Milton, Wordsworth, G M Hopkins, Ezra Pound and William Carlos Williams.

2. Find some regular poems – like the nursery rhymes and songs you used in the last chapter – and change them to introduce irregularities like caesura, spondees, pyrrhics, leading and trailing syllables, elision, substituted feet etc.

3. Try analysing an ordinary sentence. Can you make a metrical analysis of it? How much sense does it make, outside of a poem with a regular metre? Can you find interesting rhythmic effects within it? Of course, some sentences will be more interesting than others.

Study tips

1. Metre gives you a way to grasp the rhythm of a poem: rhythm is musical. Listen to different kinds of music to improve your ear for rhythm. Notice how some musical styles use very regular rhythms (dance music is like this) whereas others use loose, flexible rhythms (jazz, say) or completely irregular ones (some post-war classical music is one example).

2. Practise, practise, practise. Always keep an ear out for a verse form you could analyse – even advertising jingles can give you something to think about.

4

Homophony

One-minute summary – Homophony means 'the same sound'. The best-known form of homophony is rhyme, but there are other kinds too. Homophony is another element of poetic form. Homophony can be used regularly, as part of a poem's overall structure, or it can be used as a local variation. As with metre, the presence or absence of homophony can have an impact on what the words mean and how you interpret them. In this chapter you will learn:

▶ what homophony is
▶ the different types of homophony
▶ the relationship between homophony and structure
▶ how to do a homophonic analysis
▶ what homophony means

What is homophony?

Homophony means 'the same sound'. Words have a homophonic relationship if they share sounds in common. For example, 'sun' and 'swat' are homophonic in the sense that they share the same initial sound, 's'. So are 'walk' and 'torn', because of the vowel sounds being the same.

Homophony, like metre, is about sound, not letters. So 'sun' and 'sheet' don't have a homophonic relationship even though they begin with the same letter because they share no sounds in common.

Types of homophony
Basically, two words can share:

1. consonant sounds
2. vowel sounds
3. both

In this section you will find examples and explanations of all of the common forms of homophony.

▶ *Study tip* – If you are not sure about vowels, consonants, syllables and so on, see the section 'What metre is' in chapter 2.

Rhyme

Rhyme is the best-known of the homophonic structures used in poetry, but it is actually rather complicated.

▶ *Definition of rhyme* - Two words rhyme if the portions from the vowel sound of the last stressed syllable to the end of the words sound identical.

Example 1

That's a bit of a mouthful. Let's start with something simple, like two monosyllabic words: 'lapse' and 'maps'. These words rhyme because from the vowel sound to the end of the word they have identical sounds: 'aps'.

Example 2

Now, take a polysyllabic word: 'perhaps'. The stress falls on the second syllable: 'per-HAPS'. It rhymes with 'lapse' and 'maps' because everything before the vowel sound of the stressed syllable is ignored.

The identification of the stressed syllable is important. 'Handicaps' does not rhyme with any of these words, because the stress falls on the first syllable: 'HAN-di-caps'.

Perfect and imperfect rhymes

This is the rule for perfect rhyming. Poets sometimes use imperfect rhymes (like 'maps/handicaps') for effect – and you'll see what this might mean later. You will also sometimes find imperfect rhymes used simply because the poet was unable to find a suitable word which would make a perfect rhyme.

Remember, poets are not slavishly following a recipe when they write poems; sometimes the perfect rhyme just is not as important as exactly the right word. Complete adherence to perfect rhyming is sometimes considered a sign of unsophisticated, unimaginative writing, like greeting-card doggerel. Rhymes can certainly become clichés, as Pope remarks in his 'Essay on Criticism':

> If crystal streams 'with pleasing murmurs creep,'
> The reader's threatened (not in vain) with 'sleep'

As a vague rule, the later the poem, the more cliched lines like this will feel.

Assonance and consonance
The lead character in Willie Rushton's *Educating Rita* calls assonance 'getting the rhyme wrong', which is the truth, if not the whole truth.

▶ *A more formal definition of assonance* – The sharing of vowel sounds, but not consonant sounds.

'Torn' and 'moor' share assonance because their vowel sounds are the same, but they don't rhyme because of the 'n' sound at the end of 'torn'.

Guess what? Consonance is the sharing of consonant sounds but not vowel sounds. 'Torn' and 'mine' share consonance because of the 'n' sound they both end in, but they don't rhyme because they don't have the same vowel sounds.

Spotting assonance and consonance through collocation
Assonance and consonance are everywhere, of course, because there are only so many sounds in the English language. What

you are looking for is an effect, something which seems significant. Often this will be because the words come next to each other:

> Break, break, break
> On thy cold gray stones, O Sea!

Here the 'o' sounds in 'cold', 'stones' and, of course, 'O', are identical. It is fair to say that three identical vowel sounds in such a short line is no coincidence. This is called 'collocation' – co-location, being in the same place – and it's one way poets use assonance and consonance.

Para-rhyme

The fact that assonance and consonance are like 'getting the rhyme wrong' has led some poets – particularly in the twentieth century – to use them instead of rhyme. In general this is thought to make the poem feel discordant and un-comfortable, as in these lines by Wilfred Owen:

> It seemed that out of battle I escaped
> Down some profound dull tunnel, long since scooped
> Through granites which titanic wars had groined.
> Yet also there encumbered sleepers groaned,

Instead of the expected perfect rhymes, each pair of lines ends with a consonance. In many cases, Owen uses consonance at both ends of the words – gr-oi-n'd, gr-oa-n'd – to make it obvious that this is not just a coincidence. He also uses mainly monosyllabic words, which is a common way to draw attention to assonance and consonance.

Alliteration

Alliteration simply means starting with the same sound, like this:

> I sing of brooks, of blossoms, birds and bowers

It's usually used to draw words together. Slogans, catch-phrases, newspaper headlines and the names of products all regularly use alliteration to make several words sound unified: think of 'safe and sound', 'rock and roll' or 'Kit Kat'.

Onomatopoeia

This is a tricky one to spell; what it essentially means is words imitating non-linguistic sounds. Onomatopoeia is a kind of poetic sound effect: the word actually sounds like what it means. There are plenty of words in English which we commonly think of as onomatopoeic: splash, ding, screech, scream, flutter, slide, drip, bang and hundreds more.

Poetic onomatopoeia often uses words that we don't usually think of this way to create a sound effect. Here's Owen again:

> Only the stuttering rifles' rapid rattle
> Can patter out their hasty orisons.

This is clever stuff, because Owen uses three words which we might usually think of as onomatopoeic ('stuttering', 'rattle', 'patter'), but through alliteration he also draws in the words 'rifles' rapid'. The effect is onomatopoeic even though 'rifle' and 'rapid' aren't normally thought of as sound-effect words.

A word of warning

Students sometimes think onomatopoeia is a natural effect: the words just sound like what they mean, and that's that. In fact, it can only work though convention. That's why Owen uses conventional onomatopoeic words *and* alliteration to make sure we notice the effect. If you aren't sure whether an onomatopoeic effect is present, it's best to assume it's not, or to mention it as a possibility (this is fine: you don't have to be dogmatic about everything).

Homophony and structure

Homophony is a part of a poem's form, but so far we haven't heard much about how it affects the poem's meaning. To get to this, we'll need to look at how homophony can relate to the structure of a poem.

Rhyme schemes

The most familiar sort of homophonic structure is the rhyme scheme. This is a regular pattern of rhyming which the poet uses very much like a regular metre. Let's return for example to Shakespeare:

> Here the anthem doth commence:
> Love and constancy is dead,
> Phoenix and the turtle fled
> In a mutual flame from hence.

The first line rhymes with the fourth, and the second line rhymes with the third. This pattern is continued throughout the first section of the poem.

In more recent (late nineteenth-century onwards) poetry, like Wilfred Owen's 'Strange Meeting', which we saw part of above, assonance and/or consonance can replace rhymes, but otherwise the rhyme scheme is the only regular, structural homophony you'll find in a poem.

Blank verse

Not all poems have rhyme schemes. Many twentieth-century poets have rejected rhyme as a structural tool, but unlike metre, non-rhyming poetry has always been around. The most common sort is 'blank verse'. People sometimes think this means the same as 'free verse', but it doesn't: it specifically refers to non-rhyming iambic pentameter. Virtually all of Shakespeare's plays are written in blank verse, and the form has been very popular right up to the twentieth century. So even if a poem is fairly old, don't imagine that it must have a rhyme scheme: some (especially longer ones) haven't.

Rhyme scheme irregularities

Unlike metres, rhyme schemes tend to be extremely regular. Poets rarely use assonance or consonance instead of a full rhyme, and the result is often felt to be an imperfection rather than a deliberate effect.

Distorted pronunciation

Rhyme schemes are so regular that sometimes a poet will choose to distort the pronunciation of a word to make it fit. Look at these lines by Robert Herrick, from an erotic poem about dishevelled clothing:

> A sweet disorder in the dress
> Kindles in clothes a wantonness.
> A lawn about the shoulders thrown
> Into a fine distractiön;

According to the rhyme scheme, these are supposed to rhyme. If the umlaut (two dots) over the 'o' wasn't there, we would say that this was a rather startling homophonic *and* metrical irregularity.

Instead, though, it looks as if Herrick is trying to encourage us to pronounce it 'dis-TRAC-she-OHN'. This has two effects. In the first place, it's closer to the French pronunciation and this would have carried connotations of erotic sophistication (as it still does, to some extent, today). The second effect is one of form enacting content: the disorganised clothing which Herrick finds so exciting is enacted by this disorganised bit of poetry. Distorted pronunciation is also very often a humorous effect, something like the performance of a deliberately awkward clown, as it may be here (you would have to look at the rest of the poem to decide).

Non-structural homophony

Homophony other than rhyme is rarely used in a repetitive, predictable way; it comes up at odd moments and leaves you wondering whether or not it is relevant.

The question you should always ask yourself is *not*: Did the author intend it? but, Does it affect my understanding of the poem? You will never know what the author intended in most cases anyway, but you can look for clues to whether you're seeing a significant effect or just a random feature. The best clue is collocation: if you see several homophonic effects close together, it's likely that your attention will be drawn to them, and that in itself makes them significant.

Analysing a rhyme scheme

It is very easy to analyse rhyme schemes; you are looking for a group of lines with a structure which then repeats itself. Going step-by-step, you:

1. Identify the rhymes.
2. Look for repeated units.
3. Check for structural variations.

Identify the rhymes
Let's take 'The Phoenix and the Turtle' again:

> Here the anthem doth commence:
> Love and constancy is dead,
> Phoenix and the turtle fled
> In a mutual flame from hence.

Here, you know that 'commence' rhymes with 'hence' and that 'dead' rhymes with 'fled'. So, mark the first group of rhyming words 'A' and the second group 'B'. 'A' rhymes are those that sound like '-ence', and 'B' rhymes are those that sound like '-ed':

Here the anthem doth commence:	A
Love and constancy is dead,	B
Phoenix and the turtle fled	B
In a mutual flame from hence.	A

Look for repeated units

If the poem was only four lines long, we would be finished: we would say it rhymed ABBA. The fact is, it isn't the whole poem; there are eighteen separate stanzas in 'The Phoenix and the Turtle'. Here is the one after the one we just analysed:

> So they loved as love in twain
> Had the essence but in one;
> Two distincts, division none:
> Number there in love was slain.

You have to know that 'one' rhymed with 'none' in Shakespeare's time – or, at least, that was the poetic convention, and it's a convention which poets and songwriters still use today even though not many people pronounce these two words the same way.

Once you know that, you can see that this stanza rhymes 'CDDC' according to our analysis:

> A -ence
> B -ed
> C -ain
> D -one

But think formally for a minute. CDDC and ABBA are exactly the same things; they just mean that the fourth line rhymes with the first and the second with the third. So, if the whole poem was like this we would simply say it was written in four-line stanzas rhyming ABBA.

Check for structural variations

If there is the odd word which doesn't rhyme perfectly, you would say this was an irregularity, but you wouldn't say it was part of the form of the poem. However, it's important to check that the poem doesn't change. 'The Phoenix and the Turtle' stays with ABBA right up until the end, which goes like this:

Beauty, truth and rarity,
Grace in all simplicity,
Here enclosed in cinders lie.

Death is now the phoenix' nest
And the turtle's loyal breast
To eternity doth rest,

Leaving no posterity:
'Twas not their infirmity,
It was married chastity.

(. . . etc . . .)

The rhyme scheme is simply AAA. The first stanza seems to contain an imperfect rhyme ('RAR-i-ty' doesn't rhyme with 'sim-PLI-ci-ty' because of stress) and 'lie', which rhymes with neither. In Shakespeare's time, though, it was a convention that the ending '-ity' could be pronounced '-i-TIE' (hence 'RAR-i-TIE', 'sim-PLI-ci-TIE').

You either know this or you don't. You do now, but even if you didn't you'd guess that these were irregularities, not structural features, because of the regularity of the rest of the poem.

When there's no overall structure . . .

. . . it's sometimes possible to find repeated cells or units which might or might not give you a vague formal element and which, in turn, might or might not be useful. It's always worth checking and spending five minutes seeing what you can find.

Here's the rhyme scheme for Arnold's 'Dover Beach':

ABA C DBD C EF C GFG	(stanza 1)
ABA CBC	(stanza 2)
ABCDBEDC	(stanza 3)
ABBA CDDC C	(stanza 4)

As you can see, it has no regular pattern in terms of repeated stanzas. But it does have a tendency towards ABA-type patterns. The first stanza contains three of these and the second has two. These are then expanded into ABBA patterns for the last stanza; the third stanza seems completely random, though rhyme is still used, as if to loosely bind the lines together.

If you did your assignment at the end of chapter 1, you will know that 'Dover Beach' uses metre in a very fragmented, distorted way, but it doesn't totally ignore it. In the same way, Arnold uses fragments of a rhyme scheme in a rather disorientating manner – and one which was pretty groundbreaking for 1867.

If you know the poem's content, you might also feel that the more regular final stanza enacts the element of hope which it contains, in contrast to the panic and despair which goes before it. Could it be that Arnold's ABAs, those fragments of traditional poetic practice, are re-cast as ABBAs at the end, enacting a fresh hope in the face of chaos? That's not something you would say lightly, but in the context of an analysis it might be justified.

What homophony means

We have already seen a lot of examples of homophony being meaningful, but a recap of the most important ones will be useful. They are:

1. foregrounding
2. association

Foregrounding

As we have already seen, 'foregrounding' is just a technical term for 'drawing attention to'. Homophony can foreground words in the middles of lines, making them stand out. The absence of a rhyme where you expect one – whether it is replaced by assonance or consonance or no homophony at all

– can also foreground the guilty word just as an off-key note stands out even in a whole orchestra.

Association

To put it very simple-mindedly, words that sound like each other might *be* like each other. This is how alliteration works to bind a group of words together. Here is G M Hopkins again:

As kingfishers catch fire, dragonflies draw flame

The line is virtually broken in half at the comma because of the alliteration on each side which unifies the words (and also the caesura, which you might have spotted). This is useful to Hopkins, of course, because kingfishers aren't particularly flammable, and nor are dragonflies. The alliteration makes the image more acceptable because it makes it seem slightly more natural.

In just the same way, the advertising slogan 'My goodness, my Guinness!' attempted to make a connection between the alcoholic beverage and physical health. It was more sophisticated than the alliterative 'Guinness is good for you' (an earlier slogan) because the homophony was stronger ('My g–ness, my g–ness') and the effect more subtle. Note that the phrase 'My goodness, my Guinness' does not actually claim that Guinness has any health-enhancing properties – the suggestion is entirely done by homophony.

Tutorial

Practice questions

1. Define the following terms: rhyme, assonance, consonance, onomatopoeia, rhyme scheme, para-rhyme, blank verse.

2. What are the two main effects of homophony?

Discussion points

Is rhyme now old-fashioned, or can modern poets make interesting use of it? Try to find some examples.

Practical assignments

1. Compose a short, humorous stanza in each of the following forms: ABAB, AABA, ABBA, ABBACC, ABCDCBA, ABBCDDCAA. Then make up some forms of your own.

2. Try composing a short poem using para-rhymes instead of perfect rhymes (use any rhyme scheme you like):
   (a) using assonance only
   (b) using consonance only

3. Look for different kinds of homophony in the world around you, including brand names, newspaper headlines and advertising slogans.

Study tips

1. Remember not to be an anorak: always ask yourself what homophony *means*, once you have spotted it.

2. The more poetry you read and analyse, the better you will become at recognising what is unusual and what is common in different periods.

3. Think of any phenomenon which makes a sound and create a sentence which uses onomatopoeia to describe it. Some examples might be traffic, someone typing, a rain storm or a bird singing. Remember that you can use conventional sound-effect words and you can also draw in other words using assonance, consonance or alliteration.

5

Metaphor

One-minute summary – A metaphor is a 'figure of speech' – an unusual way of saying something. In fact, metaphors are everywhere, and being able to analyse them is an essential skill for literary critics. In a metaphor, one thing is compared with another. As well as the classic metaphor, in this chapter we will look at allegories, analogies, symbols and other figures of speech which compare two different things. We are now moving away from the purely formal elements of metre and homophony into a more sophisticated area. Metaphor *is* a formal element, but it is also very closely dependent on the content of the poem. In the previous chapters, we've analysed poetry without too much concern over what the words mean. From here on, the words will be very important indeed. In this chapter you will learn:

▶ what is a metaphor
▶ how to recognise and analyse metaphors
▶ what similes, symbols, allegories, analogies and conceits are
▶ what metaphors can mean

What is a metaphor?

In a sentence, a metaphor is a phrase which compares two different things without being completely explicit about it. A metaphor is actually composed of three parts: canon, figure and ground. By learning to analyse these, you'll learn to identify and make sense of metaphors.

Metaphor as comparison and generalisation
Dave and the pig
In a metaphor, A is compared with B as a way of saying

something about A. Let's start with a simple, everyday example: 'Dave is a pig'. We will assume that we know that Dave isn't literally a pig, and so he is being compared with one to bring out some quality he has.

Now, conventionally (and this is very unfair on pigs) these creatures have poor manners, particularly in two areas: at the table, and in matters of the heart. Let's assume that the context of the phrase tells us that Dave's eating dinner. Hence, Dave and the pig are said to be the same *in respect of their eating habits*.

Yet the phrase simply says that Dave *is* a pig. This is what a metaphor is – two things which have one feature in common are said to be identical. The two are compared, but the comparison is generalised.

Similes

In case you were wondering, a 'simile' is an explicit metaphor. If we had said 'Dave eats like a pig', then we would have used a simile. Similes are easy to analyse because they are explicit, so there is not much more to say.

Some writers claim that if we had said 'Dave is like a pig', that too would be a simile just because the word 'like' makes it explicit that a comparison is taking place. That may be so, but you still need to do the same analytical work as if it were a metaphor, so why worry about it?

If in doubt, use 'simile' where you see phrases such as 'A is like B' or 'A is as big as a B'. The word 'metaphor', in modern literary criticism, has far wider application than it used to, and 'simile' is used much less. Only the most pedantic of readers will complain if you use 'metaphor' instead of 'simile'.

Canon, figure and ground

Dave, the pig and the eating habits which unite them are the three essential parts of this metaphor. You won't be surprised to learn that there are technical terms for them: canon, figure and ground. Here they are:

Canon	Dave	The one being described
Figure	The pig	The thing used to describe the canon
Ground	The table manners	The thing which the canon and figure share

Figure 5-1

The ground is the basis for the metaphor. If Dave asked 'On what grounds are you calling me a pig?', our poet could reply, 'Your filthy eating habits'. You can change the canon or the figure, and you can even change the ground:

Canon:	Geraldine is a pig (same figure and ground)
Figure:	Dave is a monkey (okay, maybe this is a stretch, but monkeys are pretty messey eaters too)
Ground:	Dave was a pig to Geraldine (now we're talking about Dave's romantic behaviour, so the ground has changed)

Figure 5-2

Here are some more examples:

You will notice that in each case we have found something which isn't said explicitly in the phrase itself: the ground. We might also find that the figure was partly implicit, as in the 'high and dry' example; the phrase doesn't mention a boat at all.

Example	Canon	Figure	Ground
Sue was left high and dry	Sue	A shipwrecked boat	Both are helpless and abandoned
Pete ratted on his mates	Pete	A rat	The rat's conventional untrustworthiness
The week stretched out before Sally	The week	A long road	Necessary, boring task of getting from one end to another

Figure 5-3

More complex metaphors

Poetic metaphors are often more complicated than everyday ones, and this kind of analysis will reveal a fair bit of additional material. For example, here is Shelley on the state of 'England in 1819':

Rulers – leechlike to their fainting country cling

Here rulers (canon) are compared with leeches (figure), the ground being the parasitic way of life of the leech. The metaphor works especially well because leeches have negative connotations: no-one likes a leech. As well as being descriptive, Shelley's line is also insulting to the 'rulers'. You will often find that this is the case; negative figures are used for negative descriptions, and positive ones where the metaphor is supposed to be 'flattering'. Here is the Monty Python team subverting this tradition:

'My Lord is like a stream of bat's piss.'
'WHAT?'

'I merely meant, my Lord, that you shine out like a shaft
of gold when all around is dark.'

If you find inappropriate terms used like this in a serious
metaphor, always ask yourself why – there are likely to be
valuable clues hiding there.
Shelley's metaphor is connected to a second one, comparing the country (canon) to a person (figure) who the
leeches cling to. The ground is harder to find this time,
unless you know that it is very common to compare Britain
with a human body, with the king at the head and the
different regions and functions of the country as the different
parts of a body, all working together. This was known as the
'body politic' in the Renaissance, and is an idea we still use
today. When we talk about a company being 'corporate', we
are using a word derived from the Latin '*corpus*', meaning
'body'. Instead of the king being the head, the ruler is now a
leech on the body. This, as you will see in the next chapter, is
an example of irony.
That's nearly 200 words of analysis, not counting Monty
Python, from just eight words of poetry – and we haven't even
related this to the rest of the poem yet. I'm sure you are
beginning to see that a metaphor is a gift to you as a literary
critic – if you analyse it carefully.

How significant is the metaphor?
This is the question you must always ask yourself. The answer
will be, roughly, one of the following three.

Ornamental
Ornamental metaphors are just there to produce a local effect,
as the image of the sky as a vault which appears in these lines
from Tennyson's *The Lotos Eaters*:

Hateful is the dark-blue sky
Vaulted o'er the dark-blue sea
Death is the end of life; ah, why
Should life all labor be?

Here the sky is the canon, the vault the figure and the apparently dome-like shape of the sky is the ground. Whenever looking at ornamental metaphors, see whether they are related to the themes which the lines are discussing. Here the infinity of sky and sea beyond the Lotos Eaters' island are invoked to represent death; a vault is another name for a crypt, in which the dead are buried.

Thematically important
Shelley's metaphor of leeches for rulers is an important part of his theme, which is the decline of monarchy and the established order in England. It is only one of several different metaphors in the poem, but it's an important one and you would expect it to link up with the others in an interesting way.

Central
Some metaphors are really central to a poem. In most cases, these are too extended to be properly considered metaphors – next we will talk about allegories, conceits and suchlike which are essentially metaphors which have run out of control.

Step-by-step analysis
As you start practising analysis of metaphors, follow these steps. You will soon get the hang of it and be able to work in a more instinctive way.

1. Pick out the figure and canon. This should be easy enough.

2. Try to work out what the ground is. This can be more difficult and it might be conventional rather than self-evident.

3. Are the figure, canon and ground unexpected in any way? Are you surprised by any of them?

4. Is the metaphor a commonly-used cliché like 'Dave is a pig', or is it more unusual?

5. Check that this isn't two or three metaphors mixed together. If it is, separate them: this is what 'analysis' means, separating and simplifying what's obscure and complex.

6. If several metaphors are involved, ask yourself what their relationship is.

7. How does the metaphor relate to the poem as a whole?

Extensions of the metaphor

As we've seen, 'straightforward' metaphors like Tennyson's 'vaulted' sky aren't the only kind. If you're beginning to feel that metaphors like Shelley's leeches can be complicated, confusing and difficult to make complete sense of, you're right.

Metaphors are one of the things which make language as complex and open to interpretation as it is. In this section, we'll see how metaphors can get out of hand in two different ways. They can be extended to breaking point – where they become 'conceits' – or they can be flawed in their construction, when we call them 'mixed metaphors'

Conceits

Here is a simple definition of a conceit. It is a metaphor in which the figure and the canon are expanded to an extent that they are not simply 'mapped onto' each other any more. In the works of the 'metaphysical' poets like John Donne and Andrew Marvell, a single metaphor is often extended into a conceit which takes up the entire poem.

A conceit tends to be more ambiguous than a straightforward metaphor. In other words, its meaning is less clear and that means extra room for complex, more-than-meets-the-eye meanings. That, as you know, is good news for you. Here are a couple of examples.

Example 1: Shelley

In fact, Shelley's metaphor could be seen as an example of a conceit. Here it is in context:

> Rulers who neither see, nor feel, nor know,
> But leechlike to their fainting country cling
> Till they drop, blind in blood, without a blow

Instead of thinking of two metaphors, think of just the one – 'rulers are like leeches, in that they are parasitic' – extended into a whole picture. The ground is now a whole range of qualities: blindness, insensitivity, stupidity, weakness, decadence.

Interestingly – and here is what makes these lines a good candidate for being a conceit – the way the canon and the figure are expanded are quite different. The canon is given a list of qualities; the rulers can't see, feel or know. The figure, though, is given a little narrative: it clings, fills up with blood, then drops off. It's as if the canon is used for description and the figure provides a sequence of events.

This kind of independent expansion of figure and canon is a distinguishing feature of a conceit. Look out for it. Where you see it, you will find there is a lot of work to do before you make sense of it, but once you have you will be in possession of some first-rate essay material.

Example 2: Emerson

Here is another kind of conceit, taking up a whole short poem by R W Emerson, called 'Grace':

> How much, preventing God! how much I owe
> To the defenses thou hast round me set:
> Example, custom, fear, occasion slow,
> These scorned bondmen were my parapet.
> I dare not peep over this parapet
> To gauge with glance the roaring gulf below,
> The depths of sin to which I had descended,
> Had not these me against myself defended.

Again, we should look for the central metaphor, which seems to be essentially comparing God's grace with the walls of a castle, the ground being the protective value each has. The poem, though, gently turns our expectations on their heads. Whereas a castle's parapets are designed to keep an attacking enemy out, it seems that God's spiritual parapets in fact keep the narrator inside, free from temptation and the 'depths of sin'. Again, the canon and figure part company slightly: they've been extended in different directions, and they don't make a straightforward fit any more.

If I came across this poem in an 'unseen' exam, my first instinct would be to look for a problem in this situation, something which makes it less simple that it first appears. My eyes are drawn right away to the last line, which pinpoints the contradiction in the conceit: my castle protects *me* from *you*, and my prison protects *you* from *me*, but the structure which Emerson describes protects *me* from *myself*.

You might notice that the walls of God's grace are described in oddly negative terms:

> Example, custom, fear, occasion slow,
> These scorned bondmen were my parapet.

Could Emerson be using the ambiguity of the conceit to ask whether 'God's grace' is no more than social taboo, a restriction on personal freedom? Maybe: only a more extended analysis could reveal that, but identifying the conceit would be the start of the process.

Mixed metaphors

Dave, the pig and the labourer

A mixed metaphor is one, basically, which doesn't make sense. You may have come across it when listening to someone who uses a lot of clichés without thinking about them. They end up saying something like, 'David, stop shovelling your food like a pig.'

Here two metaphors have been blended into one sentence:

David is shovelling his food
David is a pig

Now, when we say someone is shovelling their food, we mean that they are eating like someone digging a hole: ungracefully and with an air of performing a laborious task. The figure is a manual worker, and for David to eat like a manual worker would simply never do.

If David is eating like a pig, though, he is unlikely to be shovelling. In fact, if David is eating like a pig then he is eating like an animal which is not sophisticated enough to use tools like shovels, knives or forks – one reason why animals have poor table-manners.

Mixed metaphors are usually contradictory, like this one. It disparages David for using a shovel (metaphorically) and for being like an animal, which can't use utensils. Yet they are also usually revealing. The speaker, without meaning to, has created a third metaphor: 'Manual workers are like animals'. That's pretty likely to surprise the person who said it, but there it is.

This is an example of what modern critical theorists sometimes call 'slippage': the tendency that language has to betray you by slipping out of control. Mixed metaphors and other 'accidental' features are one place where this slippage is often found.

Example
Here's a snippet by Swinburne, from 'The Poet and the Woodlouse', which is anything but accidental:

Man, the fleshy marvel, always feels a certain kind of awe
    stick
To the skirts of contemplation, cramped with nym-
    pholeptic weight;

Don't worry: it's a parody, and Swinburne is being deliberately confusing. Nympholepsy is a seizure brought on by an un-attainable beauty (I think Swinburne made this up). I imagine that the rest of the words are perfectly understandable, though, so why is it so hard to get at what he means?

Well, the lines are plagued by mixed metaphors. The phrase 'skirts of contemplation' seems to be a metaphor along these lines:

Canon	Figure	Ground
Contemplation	Clothing	Being "wrapped up" in one or the other

Figure 5-4

The idea of being 'wrapped up in contemplation' brings with it an image of staying still. However, the idea that awe 'sticks' to these skirts and weighs them down implies that the contemplator is trying to go somewhere and being hindered. This looks like a second metaphor:

Canon	Figure	Ground
Contemplation	A journey	The intention of reaching a conclusion: a solution to the problem being likened to the destination of a journey

Figure 5-5

Then, the idea that awe in the face of the majesty of the universe might weigh down the thinker and make it more difficult to understand her subject makes perfect sense. The two different pictures which these two lines try to conjure up – the thinker 'wrapped up in contemplation' and the thinker on a 'journey of discovery' – are both clichés. To invoke both at once, Swinburne uses a mixed metaphor which isn't just unfamiliar, it's very hard to make any sense of.

Coupled with his use of obscure words (which gets worse, not better, as the poem goes on) these lines seem foolish and pretentious. The clichés only add to the image of a narrator with little imagination or intelligence disguising the fact by means of over-complicated language.

When a metaphor isn't a metaphor

People often get the term 'metaphor' mixed up with terms like 'symbol', 'analogy' and 'allegory'. To make sure you are not one of those people, here are definitions of those terms and some brief examples.

Symbolism

A symbol is commonly defined as an 'overdetermined image', but that isn't very helpful if you don't know what 'over-determined' means. A symbol is essentially something which has a great deal of different meanings crammed into a single word or phrase.

So it's never advisable to say something like 'Oh, a lion is a symbol of bravery', in a breezy kind of know-it-all voice. Maybe, in a particular poem, a lion is being used as a figure for a brave person in a metaphor, and bravery is the ground. That would be a more exact way of putting it.

Conventionally, a lion could represent nobility, monarchy, savage nature, Christ, Richard I, England and more. That's because the lion is used as a symbol, and its meaning isn't determined by just one thing: it's overdetermined, and it can mean all sorts of different things. Learning these different conventions is something which will come with time; the more you read, the more you'll pick up. Most western European symbols come from the Bible, the Greek and Roman classics, mediaeval art and renaissance science.

Allegory

An allegory is a way of talking about one thing to mean something else. You might imagine talking about a shepherd and his sheep to explain the relationship between God and humanity as a way of making the concepts more immediate and easier to understand. Formally speaking, there are two kinds: narrative allegory and 'speaking pictures'.

The difference between allegory and metaphor is that an allegory is extended and complex, but that the figure is focussed on almost exclusively. The reader is usually expected to know what the canon is, perhaps from just a few lines at the beginning or end, and to use her/his imagination to work out how it corresponds to the figure.

Narrative allegory

A narrative allegory is easy to understand: it's a story which follows the same pattern as another story, and it's intended that the reader will find the relationship between the two illuminating. The fall of Satan from heaven, for example, was often used as an allegory for human pride and sin. Narrative allegory was a staple of mediaeval literature, and although it's never fallen into total disuse it's become less popular as literature has concerned itself less with moral instruction.

Speaking pictures and 'blazon'

A speaking picture, on the other hand, is a slightly more modern technique, developed in the Renaissance from the mediaeval practice of 'blazon'. A blazon is a way of saying in words what a heraldic crest looks like, and it proceeds by describing each part very carefully in a prescribed order. Here's Chaucer describing the Wife of Bath (in my own modern version):

> Her headscarves were very fine in texture;
> I dare say there was ten pounds in weight
> That she wore on her head on a Sunday.
> Her stockings were fine scarlet,
> Tied very straight, with soft, new shoes.

Her face was bold, fair and ruddy.
[. . .]
Gap-toothed she was, truly,
She rode at ease on an ambling horse,
Properly veiled, and on her head was a hat
As broad as a soldier's shield;
A riding skirt was around her large hips,
And on her feet were a pair of sharp spurs.

Now, this might look like a straightforward description, but look at it again: look at the meticulous detail with which Chaucer described each feature. This is a literary 'blazon', and it's full of significance. He is at pains to tell us what a modest woman she is, with her veil, straight-laced stockings and Sunday best headscarves. But he also mentions a number of things which are at odds with it - her ostentatious hat, wide hips and fair complexion (these last two were both 'sexy' features, at least in Chaucer's time) and rather aggressively sharp spurs.

This physical description reflects what goes on in the section I missed out. Chaucer's narrator mentions that she's had five husbands – then suddenly changes direction and goes on about her pious pilgrimages instead. The narrator may be shy of the fact, but his description shows her to be a vivacious, unconventional and even outrageous character.

A 'speaking picture' (the phrase is Sir Philip Sidney's) works in much the same way. It builds up fragments to produce a picture in which the overall meaning depends on the meanings of the different bits and how they are put together. You can spend a lot of time analysing a speaking picture like this. A knowledge of the poetic conventions and symbols of the time is often essential. Look out for the technique next time you see a description. Although it's a typically renaissance technique, you can even spot it in modern works now and again.

Analogy

An analogy is to an allegory what a simile is to a metaphor. By that I mean an analogy is an explicit allegory, in which each part of one thing is mapped explicitly onto another. Analogies are common in science and technology, but not in poetry. I've mentioned it here so you won't be one of those students who says, 'Oh, the Wife of Bath's physical appearance is an analogy of her moral character'. Wrong: it's a speaking picture or an allegorical description. If it were an analogy, it would be much more explicitly laid out, and each element of the 'canon' would be related to an element in the 'figure'.

Tutorial

Practice questions

1. Define canon, figure and ground.

2. What is a conceit? What is a mixed metaphor?

3. What are symbols, narrative allegories, speaking pictures and analogies? How does each differ from a metaphor?

Discussion points

1. How much metaphor do we use in our daily lives?

2. Can we control our language, or are we always in danger of 'slippage'?

Practical assignments

1. Look out for metaphors in everyday life. Advertisements and common figures of speech are both good places to start.

2. If you have access to children's books, see if any of them have allegorical narratives; many do, especially more old-fashioned ones.

3. Try writing a description of someone you know in the form of a 'blazon' or 'speaking picture'. You could use poetry or prose, and you could use a famous person as your subject if you prefer (you may find this less controversial).

4. Now try writing a narrative allegory. This is more difficult; first, think of your subject – any simple story with a moral should work quite well. Second, work out how to map on each character or moral perspective onto the elements of your own narrative. A really good allegory heightens the moral lesson of the original story without ever referring to it. Look in a newspaper for a story if you're stuck for a subject.

Study tip

Collect metaphors – whether mentally or on paper – as you read different poems. See which ones are used regularly and which are unusual or even unique.

6

Rhetorical Tropes

One-minute summary – Rhetoric is the art of fine speaking. A trope is a trick, a turn of phrase, a figure of speech which improves your performance as an eloquent speaker or writer. The rules of rhetoric were formulated in ancient Greece but they have long been a part of English poetry. In this chapter we won't be studying formal rhetoric – we will be looking at how poets actually use it and what effect it has. Identifying a rhetorical 'trope' in a poem is a useful way into analysing it. Here, we will look at all of the common tropes and a good number of less common ones. We will also see that rhetoric in general was at the centre of a controversy which has haunted English poetry ever since. In this chapter you will learn:

▶ what a trope is
▶ what rhetoric means in poetry
▶ the common tropes of metonymy and synecdoche
▶ more exotic tropes and how to analyse them

What is a trope?

A trope is a sort of formula for saying something in a certain way. Actually, a metaphor is an example of a trope. The thing is, metaphors are so important in poetry that they're really considered as something separate.

In a metaphor, instead of saying 'Dave is greedy', you say 'Dave is a pig'. Everyone knows that pigs are greedy, and everyone also knows that pigs are disgusting (supposedly, anyway). The trope intensifies your condemnation of Dave by saying he's greedy *and* disgusting, and more besides. There are many other tropes – recipes, if you like – for making a more elegant statement than the straightforward one.

A brief history of rhetoric in English poetry

The poetry which you are likely to be studying will have been written during or after the Renaissance. Before then, rhetoric was something studied by scholars, alongside logic and grammar. The following is a sketchy historical summary to help put rhetoric in context.

The Renaissance –

During the Renaissance, interest in ancient writers like Cicero and Aristotle started to increase. In the Elizabethan age, rhetorical 'devices' were highly praised for their ingenuity, neatness and downright cleverness.

But this is only one side of the coin. On the other side is the Reformation, which began very early in the English Renaissance – during the 1530s under Henry VIII. Protestantism quickly developed a tradition of 'iconoclasm', which means 'destroying images'. Paintings and sculptures were removed from Catholic churches and burned or smashed on a massive scale. Any sign of outward showiness was eventually seen as superstition.

This tendency – which quickly developed into Puritanism – also carried over into literature, where 'plain speaking' and humble simplicity were considered much more godly than the showing-off of the courtiers. To see the difference between these practices, compare George Herbert's apparently simple verses with Shakespeare's sonnets, which are full of clever turns of phrase.

– and beyond

The conflict between simplicity and rhetoric remains with us to this day. The Romantics favoured a simple approach, more in tune with their rustic ideals, while their contemporaries, the neo-classicists, looked for formal beauty in complexity. In the early twentieth century, modernists like Ezra Pound wrote densely complicated poetry, while the war poets like Wilfred Owen aimed for simpler, more visceral stuff.

It's worth bearing this conflict in mind when you study rhetoric in poetry. Sometimes you will find a poet taking one side or the other. Very often, the poet will claim to be using simple, direct speech but in fact employ many rhetorical devices (as Herbert does). This kind of self-referentiality (see below) is going to be very useful when you come to write an essay.

Synecdoche and metonymy

The most common rhetorical tropes are metonymy and synecdoche, which is a kind of metonymy.

▶ *Study tip* – You will understand this section better if you've read the section of the previous chapter called 'Canon, figure and ground'.

Synecdoche
Synecdoche is pronounced sin-eck-DOE-key. For all that it's hard to spell, the idea is really very simple. It just means using a physical part to express the whole thing. So the figure (description) is actually a part of the canon (what's described) itself. There is no need for a ground in synecdoche as there is in metaphor, because the two things are already connected.

▶ *Example* – 'All hands on deck'. In this phrase the hands of the crew are used to refer to the crew members themselves. After all, if they opened up the hatches and obediently laid just their *hands* on the deck, the Captain would be none too pleased.

The thing to look at here is which part is being used. In this example, the crew are reduced to mere hands, that is the parts that do the work. As far as the speaker is concerned, perhaps they are just units of labour, not people in their own right.

Metonymy
Synecdoche is a kind of metonymy. It is just that metonymy can be broader than just synecdoche; the figure needn't be a

physical part of the canon, it could be a quality of it or something associated with it. You could use metonymy to describe the Queen, for example:

(a) an aspect of the Queen (e.g. 'Your Highness')
(b) an object she is associated with (e.g. 'The Crown')

The literary critic David Lodge has remarked that metonymy and synecdoche are much more common in prose, while metaphor is very common in poetry. That is certainly true, but there are examples in poetry. Take for instance Coleridge's 'The ship was cheered' (from 'Rime of the Ancient Mariner'). The ship's *crew* were cheered. The ship, which belongs to the crew, is used to refer to the crew metonymically.

If in doubt as to whether a figure of speech is synecdoche or metonymy, use 'metonymy'.

Other rhetorical tropes

In this section, you will find a list of all of the rhetorical tropes commonly found in English poetry. There are many obscure ones, but you won't be expected to see and interpret them. Those in this section will give you every one you are likely to need (or, indeed, want) to know about. Even if you can't pin a name on a trope, the important thing is to be able to see it and analyse it in the context of the poem.

These tropes are divided into three groups:

1. formal tropes
2. informal tropes
3. intertextual tropes

Formal tropes

The tropes in this section are concerned with specific uses (or distortions) of grammar, word order or logic. Most are derived from classical rhetoric.

Chiasmus
Chiasmus means 'crossing over'. In the chiasmus, what is said one way is then said back-to-front: 'XY, YX'. Sometimes this is done just for effect and sometimes it is used to reverse the meaning. It is usually used, though, to indicate a close binding of the two concepts, as in Shakespeare's line:

Therefore I lie with her and she with me
    X   Y   Y   X

Innuendo
Innuendo uses something apparently innocuous to refer to something much more serious and, almost always, something negative. Here is one of Browning's characters, an embittered monk raising doubts about a fellow monk's virtue:

With Sanchicha, telling stories,
  Steeping tresses in the tank,
Blue-black, lustrous, thick as horse-hairs,
– Can't I see his dead eye glow,
Bright as t'were a Barbary corsair's?

Brother Lawrence's excitement over Sanchicha's stories can hardly be said to be a sin, but the innuendo is easy to read. The detailed description of her hair, and the gleam in his eye compared with that in a soldier's, are the two elements which give away what he's really interested in.

Litotes
To emphasise a positive statement, it can be turned into a negative one by means of litotes, often using 'no'. For example, 'that was a hard game' becomes 'that was no easy game'. The effect is extreme emphasis. Litotes can also be used to soften a very negative judgement. For example, 'she's no rocket scientist' or 'he's no oil painting'.

Meiosis
Sometimes, deliberate understatements are used to draw attention to the scale of the fact being stated. So, 'you could be right' can be an understated way of saying 'yes, obviously'. The lines of this gospel song aren't to be taken too literally:

> What do we think of Jesus?
> He's alright.

Oxymoron
Oxymorons are contradictions in terms. They were very popular in the early Renaissance, when English poets imitated Italian writers, especially Petrarch. Here is Sir Philip Sydney, commenting on its over-use by fashionable poets of his time:

> Some lovers speak when they their Muses entertain
> Of hopes begot by fear, of wot not what desires:
> Of force of heav'nly beams, infusing hellish pain:
> Of living deaths, dear wounds, fair storms and freezing
>   fires

The last line contains four oxymorons in the strict sense – an adjective (like 'living') which contradicts the noun ('death'). 'Heav'nly beams, infusing hellish pain' is contradictory enough to warrant the term too, as is 'hopes begot by fear', although you might be better off using the more general term 'paradox' for these.

Pun
Everyone knows what a pun is. It is a play on words, using one word which sounds like another, with the intention that the reader should think of the word which isn't said. If you wanted to sound clever, you could call it an implied homophony.

Rhetorical question
Likewise, this is familiar: good public speakers often ask questions which they then answer themselves. It's normally used as a way of injecting variety into a speech. Listening to or

reading one thing over an extended period might be a bit dull, but a debate or discussion is much more lively.

Rhetorical questions can seem to come from the narrator, creating an 'internal dialogue', as in this stanza of Herbert's describing fear of being arrested and executed:

> But must they have my brain? Must they dispark
> Those sparkling notions, which therein were bred?
>   Must dullness turn me to a clod?
> Yet have they left me, *Thou art still my God.*

Alternatively, they can be simply an expression of the obviousness of the answer: 'Isn't it better to – ?'.

Transferred epithet
An epithet is a descriptive phrase, and it is transferred from one thing to another. So, if you received 'an angry letter', it would be the person who wrote it – not the letter – which was really the angry party. Transferred epithets are quite common, and are closely related to metonymy.

The most common effect is that something inanimate, like a letter, seems to behave like a person, or a person seems to behave like an object. For example, 'he was a suburban little man', mean that his house, or his attitudes, were suburban. It is easy to confuse transferred epithets with metonymy. Sometimes a trope will actually be both, sometimes it will just be one or the other.

Informal tropes
The tropes in this section are looser rhetorical techniques, general 'ways of saying things' rather than technical tricks.

Bathos
Bathos means anticlimax or, literally, deflation. A pompous man slipping on a banana skin is bathetic. The trope is almost always used for comic effect, as in these lines by Swift:

The goddess from her chamber issues
Arrayed in lace, brocades and tissues

'Tissues' is bathetic because a real goddess would hardly have
to worry about blowing her nose. Bathos often uses bodily
functions and other staples of slapstick comedy to deflate what
seems to be grand, serious poetry.

Apostrophe
Apostrophe is a way of speaking either directly to the audience
or, less commonly, to some object or other. Although it isn't
like this in the play, the popular image of Hamlet's 'Alas, poor
Yorick' speech being addressed to a skull would be a familiar
example.

An apostrophe can give a special quality to the poem, but
that quality is likely to be different each time you see it. If
Hamlet really did do a speech to a skull, we might see him
literally 'staring death in the face' and conversing with it.
Perhaps the lines would be full of bravado, or maybe fear?
Who knows – in fact the speech is made to a gravedigger, and
the skull is just a prop.

Many poems are addressed to God. This is so common that,
although it is technically an apostrophe, it's easy to overlook
it. Don't. Any poem addressed to a specific listener – such as a
lover – is a form of apostrophe.

Euphemism
Euphemism, as you probably know, means using a softer
or more acceptable word or phrase than the obvious one,
for example 'doing it' for 'having sex', and 'resting' for 'being
out of work'. There are countless other euphemisms in daily
use.

Euphemisms can be used out of genuine squeamishness.
Alternatively, they can be used ironically, as a form of meiosis
(see above), for example 'working girl' for 'prostitute'.
Euphemisms can also be deliberately absurd, as in 'vertically
challenged' for 'short'.

Euphuism
Not to be confused with euph<u>em</u>ism, euph<u>u</u>ism is deliberately over-the-top floweriness or otherwise fancy writing. It is usually used as a parody, as in Swinburn's 'The Poet and the Woodlouse' which we saw earlier. Here is a whole stanza of pure euphuism (it's the woodlouse talking):

> And I sacrifice, a Levite – and I palpitate, a poet;–
>   Can I close dead ears against the rush and resonance
>   of things?
> Symbols in me breathe and flicker up the heights of the
>   heroic
> Earth's worst spawn, you said, and cursed me? look! approve
>   me! I have wings.

The fact that this is euphuism – not just utter madness – is evident from the nicely-timed bathos of the last line.

Don't make the classic mistake of claiming something is euphuistic just because you don't understand it. Make sure it is clearly an effect in the poem. Often this will be signalled by elements of absurdity, like the very fact that the poet is talking to a woodlouse in the first place.

Hyperbole
Hyperbole is a Greek word meaning exaggeration. When someone claims that they've told you 'a million times' not to do something, they are probably employing hyperbole (unless you really haven't been paying attention). The device was common in Renaissance love poetry – and remains so in modern political mudslinging.

Hyperbole is the use of an extreme phrase when the speaker feels strongly about something, and the normal words to describe the situation do not seem sufficient. Hyperbole therefore says more about the narrator's (not the poet's) feelings than about the thing in question.

Studying Poetry

Irony

'Irony' is quite hard to define. Essentially it means a reversal, particularly a reversal of the value of something. So if I win the lottery and die of a heart attack as a result, you'd say that was ironic, because winning the lottery is supposed to make you happy, but dying is sad, and so the value of the event has been reversed.

This is 'narrative irony' – in other words, ironic things happening. Here's a poem by Blake with a neatly ironic narrative:

I asked a thief to steal me a peach,
He turned up his eyes;
I ask'd a lithe lady to lie her down,
Holy & meek she cries.

As soon as I went
An angel came.
He wink'd at the thief
And smild at the dame –

And without one word said
Had a peach from the tree
And still as a maid
Enjoy'd the lady.

Of course, in the third stanza, we expect the angel to reward the thief and the lady for refusing to give in to the narrator's temptations. Instead, the angel is just as bad – in fact worse, because it is able to get what it wants by using supernatural powers.

You will also come across irony in the way a poem expresses itself. Essentially, this kind of irony is like a gentle and rather understated kind of sarcasm. The idea that the angel is 'still as a maid' (i.e. a virgin) while seducing the lady is an example of irony.

▶ *Study tip* – You will occasionally see the term 'dramatic irony' used. This does not mean the same thing as other kinds of irony. It is very simple. It describes the situation in which a character on stage is unaware of some crucial fact known to the audience. You are unlikely to find dramatic irony used in this way in poetry.

Pathetic fallacy

'Pathos' means 'sympathy'. The 'pathetic fallacy' is a particularly Romantic technique, in which the natural world is described as if it had human characteristics and, particularly, human emotions. Generally it is achieved by means of a metaphor or a transferred epithet. Think for example of 'the raging sea' or 'threatening rain clouds'. The effect is normally that the natural surroundings comment on or reflect whatever else is going on. Think of thunder storms in corny horror movies, in which the very forces of nature seem to close in and threaten the hapless victims.

Here is Tennyson, describing the island of the Lotos Eaters:

All around the coast the languid air did swoon,
Breathing like one that hath a weary dream.

Sometimes, in poetry, it's as if the thunderstorm is the whole film, with just a few brief scenes to hint at what it's supposed to reflect. In cases like this, it's often working like an extended metaphor or conceit (see chapter 5).

Personification

Personification is much like pathetic fallacy, but it works slightly differently. Here, something abstract (like death) is turned into a character (like Death, the 'grim reaper'). This makes it easier to say things about that subject. In that sense, personification can be like a miniature allegory (see chapter 5), or it can be part of a larger allegory.

Don't use 'personification' to refer to effects which are actually achieved by means of pathetic fallacy. You are looking for a fully-drawn physical character who is used to represent some abstract idea or other.

Anthropomorphism
This is pretty much the same as personification, except that instead of an abstract idea, the subject is an object or animal. Disney films thrive on anthropomorphism (Mickey Mouse, Dumbo the Elephant), as do many children's stories and poems.

Intertextual tropes

Intertextuality is a fancy term meaning a relationship between the poem and some other text. It names a special set of rhetorical tropes which many modern literary critics are particularly interested in.

In all but the last case, spotting intertextual tropes depends on whether you know the other text. For this reason, poems which use them heavily tend not to appear in 'unseen' exams. If it's for coursework, your edition of the poems ought to contain a footnote which will help you. Otherwise, you may have to do some digging in the library.

Literary allusion
Allusions are references to other pieces of writing, often other works of literature. As well as showing off the writer's knowledge – especially if the work alluded to is obscure – it also flatters the reader who understands it. But beyond these simple effects, a literary allusion claims a connection between the poem and the work alluded to. What impact the allusion has will depend on both works.

An allusion is not always direct or explicit. You might not spot it, or you might not be able to decipher it. Don't worry, you won't be alone, but the more you read around the better your chances are of identifying allusions and working out why they are there.

Quotation

The fact that a poem contains a quotation won't always be obvious. For example T S Eliot's 'The Waste Land' is full of quotations, but if you didn't know where they came from you could easily assume that Eliot had written them himself. Like allusion, the effect of quotation depends completely on what has been quoted. Often, though, you will find books quoted as authorities, used to back up the narrator's argument. In that case the quotation will often, but not always, come from the Bible or from the Greek or Latin classics.

Parody

You parody something by imitating it, in order to reveal its inherent absurdities. There are plenty of examples of parody in Pope's writings. You will find a few in this book. Again, if you've read enough, you will understand what is being parodied. If not, you will have some difficulties. Normally, though, a poem will parody a whole style or school of writing rather than an individual, and so a basic, broad knowledge will normally see you through.

Self-referentiality

This final element of intertextuality happens when a poem refers to itself. Sometimes this is done explicitly, and then it's likely to be an important theme. For example, many Renaissance poems claim that they will outlive their author and so make him, his ideas, or the subject of his poem (usually a lover), immortal.

Some literary critics claim that all poetry is self-referential, and that analysis can show that writing is a theme of every single poem. That may be an exaggeration, but not a great one. Always be on the lookout for hints that a poem is asking questions about writing, poetry, language, communication or meaning, even if its theme seems on the surface to be something completely different. There are *always* points to be scored from spotting self-referentiality in a poem which isn't obviously about itself.

Tutorial

Practice questions

1. Define: rhetoric, trope, oxymoron, transferred epithet, apostrophe, hyperbole, irony, and pathetic fallacy.

2. Explain the difference between:

    (a) metonymy and synecdoche
    (b) chiasmus and syllepsis
    (c) innuendoes and puns
    (d) litotes and meiosis
    (e) euphemism and euphuism
    (f) bathos and pathos
    (g) personification and anthropomorphism.

Points for discussion

1. Why do people use rhetoric? Is it more honest to avoid it?

2. Is a poem a work of art if it doesn't use any rhetoric at all?

Practical assignment

Create your own examples of each rhetorical trope, either in poetic or prose form.

Study tips

1. Don't try to memorise all these terms now. Use this chapter for reference, and whenever you think you've seen a trope that's defined here, have a look. Eventually, they will stick in your mind.

2. The most important thing isn't to remember the terms, but to get familiar with this way of analysing poems. So, if you come across a trope which isn't exactly like one of those defined here, you'll have the confidence to analyse it for yourself.

7

Genre and Style

One-minute summary – Genre and style both describe the way a poem is written. Genre describes the broad category that the poem fits into, and is often quite formal. Style deals more with the feel of the writing, and can be quite individual to a poet or even a particular poem. After the hard analytical stuff of the preceding chapters, this will probably feel like light relief: and armed with those skills, you will be in a better position to say something constructive about it. In this chapter you will learn:

▶ what genre and style are
▶ the main genres of English poetry
▶ the most common styles and how to identify them

What are genre and style?

Genre and style are rarely much use as analytical points. They are too vague and not formal enough to give you anything solid. What they *can* do is give you a 'way into' a poem, a way of approaching it and starting to think about what it is doing. Knowing about genre and style is particularly useful in 'unseen' exams, but it will be of value to you however you study poetry. Note that these categories are based on British and American poetry, although they are applicable to some extent throughout Europe, too.

Genre

Think of Hollywood movies. You probably already know a lot about genre in that area. A film genre is a broad category – disaster films, romances, epics, thrillers, action movies, comedies, westerns, science fiction and so on. There are also films which don't really fit into any of these categories –

they're often thought of as 'art' films or 'experimental' films, like David Lynch's *Blue Velvet* or Cronenberg's *Naked Lunch*.

Genres are loose, flexible categories which affect both content and form. For example an action film has a certain type of subject-matter (content), such as a simple moral conflict resolved through violent action. It will also have some formal features, like chase sequences, fights, an overall 'fast pace' and a single narrative thread (often with a romantic sub-plot).

Not all action movies fulfil all of the requirements. James Bond films, and the *Die Hard* series, are examples of films which fit the bill pretty closely. Tarantino's *Pulp Fiction*, though, has all the formal features without the simple moral conflict usually found in action movies. Indeed, the term 'generic' often means 'unimaginative'. Using genre conventions loosely is a skill which only more experienced directors can usually do effectively.

When you are looking at genre in poetry, you will likewise only find vague guidelines, rules of thumb which give you an idea of the kind of poem which you are looking at.

Style

If 'genre' is a vague term, 'style' is even vaguer. It describes the way a poem is written. Think films again. Ridley Scott's *Alien* and Paul Verhoven's *Starship Troopers* are both films in the science fiction genre, but done in very different styles.

Scott makes *Alien* into a murky, slowly-paced film peopled by quite realistic characters, using techniques from the horror genre and the fly-on-the-wall documentary. *Starship Troopers*, however, is a slick, glossy film which borrows heavily from war films and 1980s teen movies. The characters are deliberately two-dimensional and the dialogue is stilted and full of clichés.

These films are within the same genre, but have radically different styles, styles which we, as cinema-literate viewers, can immediately recognise even if we can't put names to them.

Some common genres in English poetry

Epic

The epic is one of the earliest genres in English poetry. If something is written in epic form, it means exactly that. It is done on a grand scale, dealing with big, important events, which are often either historical or based on legend. Epic poems take the form of a narrative (story), often about a single person or place. They are usually in a simple metrical form, because they are always very long – if it doesn't take up a whole book, it probably isn't an epic.

Examples of epic poems include:

(a) Homer's *Iliad*, about the siege of Troy
(b) Dante's *Divine Comedy*, about his journey through Hell, Purgatory and Heaven
(c) Milton's *Paradise Lost*, about the expulsion of Adam and Eve from the Garden of Eden.

Epics tend to be older poems. From about the seventeenth century onwards, interest in writing epics waned and even the long poems tend to have different subjects and concerns. Unless you are studying a specific epic poem, you are unlikely to come across any, just because they are so lengthy.

Ballad

A ballad is, if you like, a poor man's epic. Ballads are not as long as epics, but they are written in simple metrical form. Some ballads deal with great affairs such as kings and legendary figures. However, they can also concern themselves with the lives of more ordinary people. The older ballads were originally memorised and transmitted orally. They typically tell simple stories and, like modern journalism, they often try to avoid making moral judgements or comments.

'Ballad form' is a term used to describe the metrical form which was most popular for ballads. This consists of four-line stanzas (called quatrains), usually rhyming ABBA, ABAB or ABCB. The rhythm is typically 'eights and sixes' – in other words alternating tetrameter and trimeter, in iambs or trochees. Here is an iambic example:

The wind doth blow today,
   my love, | ᴗ / | ᴗ / | ᴗ / | ᴗ / |
And a few small drops of rain;   – ᴗ | ᴗ / | ᴗ / | ᴗ / |
I never had but one true love, | ᴗ / | ᴗ / | ᴗ / | ᴗ / | .
In cold grave she was lain. | ᴗ / | / ᴗ | ᴗ / |

The regularity of rhythms is typical of a ballad stanza, as is the rather maudlin subject-matter. Notice how the reversion of the second syllable in the last line puts a strong emphasis on 'grave' (by creating a caesura after it). This is a very useful technique if the poem is being read aloud, since it is important for the audience to grasp that the narrator's 'one true love' is dead.

When analysing a ballad, see whether it is trying to make a moral point from the story or, as is more common, just telling the story 'straight'. If the latter, see if you can find any judgements hiding in the way it is told. People didn't tell these stories for no reason: they were relevant to they way they lived. They often referred to attitudes or events which the ballad does not even mention. You won't usually be able to work out the details for yourself, but you can get a flavour for the judgements which go with them.

Elegy

An elegy is essentially a poem about someone who has died or, by extension, about death. Any poem which describes itself as 'in memoriam' (in memory of) someone-or-other is an elegy. Many elegies helpfully have the word 'elegy' in their title.

An elegy typically – indeed generically– takes the form of a poem about someone who has died recently, normally a friend of the poet. It will contain information about that person – wholly positive, of course. This part of an elegy is not much different from an obituary in a newspaper.

▶ *Key point* – The crucial difference is that a poetic elegy expands on this individual death to meditate on death and mortality in general.

It is here that you will start to find interesting things to say. Tennyson's very long 'In Memoriam' is an example, as is Milton's more manageable 'Lycidas'. Some elegies, just like action movies, do not fulfil their generic rules entirely. Thomas Gray's 'Elegy Written in a Country Churchyard', for instance, dispenses with an individual death and goes straight on to ponder death itself. Other poems may be vaguely about death, but you might not want to call them elegies exactly. In that case, you can still describe them as being 'elegiac', which means elegy-like.

Ode

'Ode' is one of the hardest words to define in English poetry. It is derived from Greek, but the Greek meaning is not relevant to English poetry as it was exclusively a dramatic technique.

Basically, an ode is like an elegy, but it isn't about death. It is a poem which starts out being about something specific (often fairly trivial), and develops into something more profound. John Keats was fond of writing odes, taking subjects like a nightingale or a Grecian urn and using them as a basis for reflections on the beauty of life.

Use the word 'ode' if the poet does; otherwise, you may want to avoid it. Note that Gray's poem about the death of his cat is called an ode, not an elegy. The elegy was a form of high, serious poetry, and to write an elegy about a cat might have seemed rather impertinent.

Sonnet

Now, a sonnet is something you can get your teeth into. If you are studying English poetry, you will get an opportunity, because nearly every poet has written at least one or two sonnets.

All sonnets have fourteen lines, and there are three kinds:

1. Petrarchan sonnets
2. Shakespearean sonnets
3. other kinds of sonnets

A sonnet is short and pithy. It involves a twist in the meaning which often gives it an unexpected shift. This part is called the 'turn'. Sonnets are very often in iambic pentameter, but not always.

Traditionally, sonnets have been romantic. When an Elizabethan gentleman wrote love poems to his lady, it was odds on they would be sonnets. That association has stayed with us, but in the centuries since Shakespeare sonnets have been written on all kinds of subjects. Sonnets should always be clever or ingenious and, if appropriate, witty. The sonnet was originally a fairly light form of verse, certainly not suited to writing elegies or epics (it is too short for that, anyway).

Petrarchan sonnets
These consist of eight lines, then six lines. The turn happens in the middle. Petrarch was an Italian poet who pioneered sonnet form and made it popular throughout Europe. These sonnets are often printed with a blank line between the two sections, which are called the 'octave' (eight lines) and the 'sestina' (six lines). Here is one of John Milton's poems about losing his sight. Instead of a blank line, this version uses indentations:

When I consider how my light is spent
    Ere half my days, in this dark world and wide,
    And that one talent which is death to hide
    Lodged with me useless, though my soul more bent
To serve therewith my maker, and present
    My true account, lest he returning chide;
    'Doth God exact day-labour, light denied?'
    I fondly ask; but Patience to prevent
That murmur, soon replies, 'God doth not need
    Either man's work or his own gifts; who best
    Bear his mild yoke, they serve him best. His state

Is kingly. Thousands at his bidding speed
And post o'er land and ocean without rest:
They also serve who only stand and wait.'

The octave describes Milton trying to continue writing, as he knows it's a sin to waste his God-given talent, but complaining that God has made it much more difficult by making him blind. In the sestina, however, Patience is personified and explains to him, essentially, that the inner, spiritual life is the most important, and that his outer works are secondary. So, the sestina contradicts the octave, which is quite proper, as in the octave the poet is complaining about God, and in the sestina he gets his answer.

▶ *Enjambment* – Notice the 'enjambment' between lines eight and nine. Enjambment is the technique of running a sentence across two or more lines. It has two effects. First, it makes the sentence feel fragmented. Second, it creates a sense of formal continuity between the lines themselves. In this case, it seems designed to give some continuity to the two sections of the poem.

Notice the way the octave divides into two groups of four lines, and the sestina into two groups of three – that too is frequently done.

Shakespearean sonnets
The Shakespearean sonnet is exactly like the Petrarchan version, except that the turn only comes between lines twelve and thirteen. In effect, this means there are three groups of four-line units (usually rhyming ABAB), and then a rhyming 'couplet' (pair of lines) at the end. In the Shakespearean sonnet, the turn is less of a dramatic change, more of a summing up of what has gone before:

When I do count the clock that tells the time,
And see the brave day sunk in hideous night;
When I behold the violet past prime,

And sable curls, all silvered o'er with white;
When lofty trees I see barren of leaves
Which erst from heat did canopy the herd
And summer's green all girdled up in sheaves,
Borne on the bier with white and bristly beard,
Then of thy beauty do I question make,
That thou among the wastes of time must go,
Since sweets and beauties do themselves forsake
And dies as fast as they see others grow;
And nothing 'gainst time's scythe can make defense
Save breed, to brave him when he takes thee hence.

Here the first quatrain (four lines) describes the cycle of nature turning from life to death. The second takes the same subject, but transforms it into the image of an old man's funeral. The third quatrain refers to the woman to whom the poem is addressed, explaining how her beauty too must eventually pass away. The final couplet is called an 'heroic couplet'. This is a self-contained, rhyming pair of lines. In this example it makes the general point that the only way to cheat death is to have children ('breed') who will outlive you.

This has quite a twist – in fact, it almost has two turns. The hangover from Petrarch can still be felt in the dramatic change from the second quatrain to the third (equivalent of the change from octave to sestina). The final couplet, though, reveals that this is not an elegiac poem about the way that all things wither and turn to dust: it's a sixteenth-century chat-up line. We can't beat death alone, so we'd better make babies instead.

Other kinds of sonnets
If a poem has fourteen lines, all of about the same length, and it has a 'twist' or 'turn' somewhere, you are probably justified in calling it a sonnet. There have been all kinds of sonnets written, with many variations.

There have even been poems written with more or fewer than fourteen lines, but claiming to be 'sonnets'. If something says it is a sonnet, fine; you can look at which features it shares with traditional forms and which it does not. Otherwise, the only one you really need to be aware of for study purposes is G M Hopkins' 'curtal' sonnet. This has six lines, a turn, and then four and a half ('God's Grandeur' is an example). Only Hopkins used the form.

Lyric

We are back once more in vaguer territory. Of course, you already know what lyrics are: the words to a song. In poetry a 'lyric' is a poem which was originally set to music or, in later pieces, one having a lyrical quality.

Ah, there's the problem. What *is* a lyrical quality? The truth is, the phrase doesn't mean much. A poem which is properly described as a 'lyric' has the following features:

(a) regular metre - but often variable stanza-lengths and rhyming
(b) a rhyme scheme of some sort
(c) subject – love, or some trivial matter, not usually a story, and not death or religion
(d) content – often focuses on the narrator's emotional response to the subject.
(e) often a chorus or 'refrain' – repeated line or lines

A lyric and an ode are therefore quite similar. In fact, an ode is often said to be an example of lyric poetry. As you can see, 'lyric' is a very loose term which you may prefer not to use unless the poet does.

The very short poem

Very short poems are interesting. You can see the whole thing in a single glance, and the challenge is to read the details closely enough to be able to write a whole essay on it. Because they have so few words in them, they tend to be 'elliptical'. That is, they imply something rather than say it outright.

Epitaphs

There was (and still is, to some extent) a tradition of poets writing epitaphs for other poets who they admired. Since they are supposed to be like carvings on gravestones, even if they weren't actually used for that purpose, they tend to be short. Here is Herrick, 'Upon Ben Jonson':

> Here lies Jonson with the rest
> Of the poets; but the best.
> Reader, would'st thou more have known?
> Ask his story, not this stone.
> That will speak what this can't tell
> Of his glory. So farewell.

This is a typical example. Don't call epitaphs 'elegiac'. It is obvious they are about death, and they aren't long enough to develop into meditations on death the way that elegies do. In fact, this one picks up on a common theme in Elizabethan poetry – the writer's attempt to make himself immortal by means of his writing.

Limericks

Another short form is the limerick. This is a humorous poem rhyming AABBA, with three long lines and two short ones. As in this example from Edward Lear, the acknowledged master of the form, short lines are sometimes run together:

> There was an Old Man with a beard,
> Who said, 'It is just as I feared! –
> Two Owls and a Hen, four Larks and a Wren,
> Have all built their nests in my beard!'

Metrically, limericks are actually rather complicated, as you'll find if you analyse this example, but they almost always have the same metrical structure.

Epigrams and other forms
There are many other short poems which don't fit either the epitaph or limerick genre. One such is the epigram. This combines a single heroic couplet (i.e. two rhyming lines) with a simple, often witty message. Here is Alexander Pope:

> Nature, and Newton's laws, lay hid in sight;
> God said *'Let Newton be!'* and all was light.

You will also find similar pithy, short observations in other metrical forms. You can call them 'epigrammatic'.

The short form is particularly popular with twentieth century poets, and the ancient Japanese art of haiku (fourteen syllables spread over three lines) was revived by the Modernists. People have always written short poems, however. The trick is to always ask yourself first: is this a witty little joke or a delicate, suggestive poem?

Complaints and apologies

The complaint
You may occasionally come across poems with the word 'complaint' or 'apology' in the title. A 'complaint' was a mediaeval poem characterised by a lot of moaning about how lousy life is, normally because of unrequited love. Like an ode or elegy, a decent complaint expands on its subject to cover something supposedly universal or at least not something personal. The word mostly fell into disuse after the sixteenth century.

The apology
An 'apology', on the other hand, is not quite how it sounds. It is usually a defence, an argument in favour of something which is maybe not fashionable at the time of writing. It's another term which hasn't really been used since the Renaissance. *Apologia* is another one of those Greek words they liked so much then. A modern example is Geoffrey Hill's deliberately nostalgic 'An Apology for the Revival of Christian Architecture in England'.

Some common styles in English poetry

There are more styles than we can possibly list in a short book like this, but these are some of the most important ones you are likely to come across.

Pastoral

'Pastoral' refers to a romantic and idealised image of the countryside – shepherds idly playing pipes and gazing at their sheep, that sort of thing. An alternative word is 'bucolic', which refers particularly to shepherds, who feature prominently in pastoral poetry. Any verse about idyllic, slow-paced rural life which doesn't mention any of the grubby bits, or the hard work that farming really involves, is pastoral.

The pastoral style was popular in the Renaissance (see Edmund Spenser's long poem, 'The Shepherd's Calendar'). It had a resurgence in the Romantic period – William Blake's poem 'The Shepherd' which we saw in chapter one is an example. Its deliberately crude structure and use of simple vocabulary presumably shows how city-dwelling poets thought rural folk spoke. The pastoral can seem quite patronising in that way.

Naivety and primitivism

The modern versions of pastoral are naivety and primitivism. Primitivism refers to the early twentieth century tendency to re-evaluate the works of other cultures (i.e. so-called 'primitives') and to borrow ideas from them. Naivety, on the other hand, tends to be a reaction against contemporary 'cleverness', a desire for simple and direct expression. You can have a single line in a poem which is deliberately naïve; the effect is often bathos (see chapter 6).

Romanticism

Romanticism is one of the big styles of poetry. As a movement it lasted from about 1780 to 1830, and took in Blake, Wordsworth, Byron, Keats, Shelley and Coleridge along with many lesser-known writers. Notice the capital 'R' in the word

Romantic. It has little to do with 'romantic' fiction of the Mills & Boon variety. The key features of Romantic poetry are:

1. Hostility towards 'establishment' institutions like the Church of England and the monarchy.

2. Emotion and individual feelings matter more than reason and moral rules.

3. Unconscious experiences (like dreams) are explored with more interest than ever before.

4. Reverence of nature: 'new age'-style mysticism about natural forces, and strong anti-technology tendency. This is more sophisticated than in the pastoral style.

Romanticism was inspired by German philosophy, especially the work of Schiller and Schlegel. They claimed that there was a strong antagonism between:

Romantic art	Classical art
Emotion	Reason
Nature	Technology
Self-expression	Formal invention
Passion	Calm

Figure 7-1

Now, I'm sure you can see that this is over-simplified nonsense. So here is your way into Romantic poetry: look to see how the poet tries to establish a Romantic way of writing, and look for the ways this doesn't work out. The best example would be complex formal patterns, or use of rhetorical tropes. Your aim is not to prove Romanticism wrong – it is to show that a particular poem is more interesting than this sort of diagram makes it sound, because it is more complex and ambiguous.

Neo-classicism

Neo-classicism was the other side of the coin to Romanticism. The neo-classical style was influential on poets from the Augustans like Pope and Dryden through to Victorians like Swinburne and even beyond. In each case, the writer has taken the formal styles of certain ancient Latin poets and applied it to English poetry. The aim was to create work which was rational, serene and which would stand the test of time, for example like that of Virgil.

Typical characteristics of the neo-classical style are:

(a) allusions linking the poem with the classical tradition
(b) complex formal schemes
(c) avoidance of personal feelings

Again, the thing to look for is the way the poem turns out to be interesting despite these neat little theories – the way, for example, that formal complexity gets out of control, or the way Romantic ideas about nature and poetic inspiration lurk in the background.

Vernacular

The vernacular style is sometimes referred to as 'dialect'. This style runs from the dialect poems of Robbie Burns right through to contemporary black American writing. Anything which uses obscure slang and/or dialect features such as non-standard pronunciations could be described as vernacular. Strictly, vernacular means 'of the common people', so you might prefer to use 'dialect' instead. To be really trendy, you could use the term 'ebonics' for black American dialect poetry, though the term is not liked by everyone.

You might find dialect poems difficult to understand. Try – in your head – adopting the right accent: this often helps.

Impressionism

This term is taken from nineteenth century painting. Impressionism in poetry is essentially an extension of Romanticism. You may like to use the term wherever descriptions aim at capturing what it is like to experience an object, rather than just describing what the object is. The technique in painting is very unrealistic. Paintings by Monet, for example, don't look anything like photographs, but try instead to capture the impression of light and colour on the eye.

Nature poems often use this style. G M Hopkins wrote much that could be called 'impressionistic'. Here he describes a bird in flight:

> I caught this morning morning's minion, king-
> dom of daylight's dauphin, dapple-dawn-drawn
> Falcon, in his riding
> Of the rolling level underneath him steady air

'I saw a bird this morning' would be clear and accurate. Hopkins opts instead for trying to create an impression of the bird's flight and, especially, the movement of the air. Often, you won't be asking yourself, 'Is it impressionism or is it Romanticism?' because it will be both.

Surrealism

Surrealism was a twentieth century movement. The surrealists were influenced by Sigmund Freud's theory of psychoanalysis, and particularly his 'discovery' of the subconscious, a dark area of the mind normally closed off, but which comes to the surface when the conscious mind loses control – typically when we are asleep. Surrealists aimed to use symbols in the same way as dreams. Symbols may mean little on the surface, but can trigger associations in the reader's mind.

Avoid saying that a particular line or image is 'surreal': say it is 'surrealist', and only do so if you are pretty sure that the poem as a whole works this way. Some students are tempted to describe any unusual metaphors or ideas as 'surreal'. Don't be one of them.

▶ *Study tip* – If you find yourself studying a number of surrealist poems, read an introduction to Freud and also C G Jung. It will help you talk intelligently about the subject.

Modernism and vorticism

This is another very important style. If you are studying English poetry, you will find it hard to avoid modernism, and quite rightly so. A few of the most important modernist poets are Ezra Pound, T S Eliot and Sylvia Plath. Key features of the modernist style are:

(a) probably written between 1890 and 1920

(b) free verse – no regular metrical structure

(c) no regular rhyme scheme

(d) very intellectual – aimed at highly educated readers

(e) the subject is often the decline of civilisation, the loss of religion and even the 'death' of poetry itself

(f) surrealist techniques were used by many modernist writers – others preferred to plunder older works for quotations and allusions

Modernism was experimental poetry, and thought of itself as on the 'cutting edge' of European literature. The modernists thought that only a minority of people would be able to understand it. Modernism was often accompanied by the attitude that everything old should be discarded and poetry completely reinvented. The result, it was hoped, would be a completely new, pure poetic style.

Vorticism

Vorticism was a movement within modernism. It especially prized modern technology. It celebrated cities, cars, trains and even mechanised warfare. Vorticists loved the energy and power of the modern world, and saw in it a hope that Europe would progress beyond the stagnation which they saw at the end of the nineteenth century. Some modernist poets sympathised with the Nazi movement, which likewise prized technology and progress. During the early years of modernism, Hitler was still painting houses, although a continuing attachment to Nazism as the century progressed becomes difficult to excuse. Vorticism was a very important force in modernism; take a look at Wyndham Lewis' writings for some examples.

▶ *Genre or style?* – You will have noticed that modernism is defined as much by content as by form. In that sense, it is halfway to being a genre rather than a style. You could write an elegy in a modernist style, but you would be hard pushed to manage a ballad, and a limerick would be pretty much impossible.

Postmodernism

The term 'postmodernism' began to be applied to literature around the early 1970s, and people still use it today. Instead of chasing after modernist purity (think of all those big geometrical paintings, or the concrete cubes which modernist architects excitedly built in the 1940s), postmodernists tend to say, 'Anything goes'.

Actually, it's not as simple as that. Postmodern poems use a collage of different poetic styles, for example mixing up traditional metrical systems, free verse and even prose in a single piece of writing. Next time you are in a city centre, take a look at a big, recently-built shopping mall. Such buildings often use a variety of architectural styles, such as corporate glass and steel, gothic window frames and Victorian industrial girders. That's one aspect of postmodernism: all styles become possible.

Postmodernists tend to be a cheerful lot. Instead of worrying about atheism and the decline of civilisation (like modernists), they celebrate the wide range of different styles and techniques which become available to you if you don't dedicate yourself to any one in particular. So in post-modernist writing you'll find a lot of pastiche (parody), kitsch (deliberate cheesiness) and so on. Of course, all of these techniques have been used in other kinds of poetry, so for safety's sake just use the term for poems written in this style after about 1970.

Tutorial

Practice questions

1. What is style? What is genre? What is the difference between them?

2. Define the terms epic, ballad, elegy, ode, lyric, epitaph and epigram.

3. Define a sonnet. Explain the differences between the Petrarchan and Shakespearean versions.

Points for discussion

1. Do poets always write in an identifiable style, or are some poems completely idiosyncratic, unlike any other in terms of style? Make sure you refer to examples in your discussion.

2. Are poems written without any genre usually more interesting than 'generic' ones? Or does the genre enable the poet to do something complex within it? Use examples and be specific.

Practical assignments

1. Many of the names of different poetic styles also apply to styles of painting. Take a trip around a large art gallery and look out for examples of pastoral, Romantic, neo-classical, impressionist, surrealist, naïve, primitivist, modernist, vorticist and postmodern painting. Tagging along with a guided tour can be very helpful, and your

resulting knowledge will im- prove your understanding of what these terms mean.

2. Music from different periods, and in different styles, can also help give you a rounded sense of a particular artistic style. Try comparing Renaissance poetry with the formal cleverness and light wit of Haydn and Mozart. Romantic composers included Brahms, Bartok and Wagner, and their music sounds much murkier and more 'emotional'. For modernism, give Boulez, Xenakis or Stockhausen a listen, and for postmodernism you might like to try the 'cut and paste' approach of John Zorn. Music by most of these composers should be available in any public library which carries recordings. Note, though, that musical styles and their literary equivalents didn't always happen at the same time; indeed, music has tended to lag behind poetry in the past. The liner notes which accompany classical recordings are often very helpful in this respect.

Study tips

1. Find anthologies of poetry in each style. Some will be easier to find than others. Quickly read through them to get a 'feel' for the style in question. You will only get this by reading large volumes of material, but you don't have to study everything in detail. This will pay big dividends if you have to sit 'unseen' exams.

2. Remember, always look for what effect a genre or style has on the *meaning* of a poem. It's not much use to simply observe that it's a Romantic elegy; use this as a way of digging into the poem.

8

Structural Analysis

One-minute summary – For a while, 'structuralism' was a major force in literary criticism. It has since become less fashionable, but it did provide some very useful techniques for analysing poetry in a completely fresh way. Structural analysis focuses on the content, but treats it formally. That might seem pretty obscure now, but all will become clear. There are two basic kinds: narrative structure and thematic structure. We'll look in detail at thematic structure, since this is more applicable to poetry. In this chapter you will learn:

▶ what structuralism is.
▶ how to analyse thematic structure
▶ how to use structuralist techniques in your own analyses

What is structuralism?

'Structure' can mean all kinds of things in literary criticism, but since the 1950s there has been an extra meaning which is quite technical. Let's take a moment to look at the background to this. It might seem a bit obscure: it is, and a handful of paragraphs is nowhere near enough to get to the bottom of it. Still, hopefully you will get a flavour of what structural analysis is all about.

Language

Ferdinand de Saussure's book *Course in General Linguistics* shook the world. It is a structural account of how language produces meaning out of sounds or marks on bits of paper. It was not the first, but it is by far the most influential.

Saussure argued that a word does not mean anything by itself. The word 'green', for example, does not have anything inherently green about it. A word only has a meaning because it is a part of a whole language, and a language is a kind of system, or structure.

So, 'green' has meaning in relation to *other* words. 'Green' really means 'the colour in between yellow and blue in the spectrum'. And, you guessed it, 'yellow' and 'blue' have similar meanings. In other words, *all meaning is relative to other words.*

After all, if someone asked you to define 'green', how would you do it? You would use other words, wouldn't you? Sure, you could point to something green, and hope the listener got the right idea, but that's not the point. It seems the most natural thing in the world to define words using other words, and that's because that's how they really get their meanings.

This can make you a bit dizzy if you think about it. All the ins and outs would take a while to go through, but you can see the general idea. A word gets its meaning from the place it occupies in the overall structure we call 'the English language'.

Myths

Anthropologist Claude Lévi-Strauss picked up on de Saussure's ideas and tried to apply them to the study of myths and legends. The result – his three-volume *The Raw and the Cooked* – is a masterpiece of twentieth century academic writing.

Lévi -Strauss took mythic stories and broke them down into their main bits. He then treated them exactly the way de Saussure treated the words in a language - as if the myth as a whole were a structure, and each part only gained meaning in relation to the others.

. . . and then everything else . . .

It might all sound like a smart-aleck exercise, but the results are pretty impressive, and they inspired literary critics to try the same thing. Structuralism was picked up by virtually every branch of the humanities and the social sciences at one time or another, and it has now been abandoned by almost all of them. The main problem is that things just don't seem to work that way. The world isn't really a closed, static structure which you can map out.

What has been left over, though, is something very useful: a whole set of techniques and ideas which you can use in your own analyses. You don't have to understand structural linguistics or anthropology to use these techniques – you just need to know how they work.

A word of warning

Structural analysis is a powerful tool. Use it with care. Avoid anything which isn't justified by the words on the page. It is easy to get carried away and start analysing structures instead of poems. Never do that: your readers will spot it a mile away and will not be impressed.

Binary oppositions

In any kind of structural analysis, 'binary oppositions' are central. A poem invariably contains many binary oppositions. Being able to analyse them will often prove extremely helpful even if you don't take your structural analysis any further than that.

What is a binary opposition?

A binary opposition is a pair of terms which are opposites. It is a loose definition. All of these examples are binary oppositions, even though some are 'opposite' in quite different ways from others:

Black	White
True	False
Man	Woman
Life	Death
Rich	Poor
Poetry	Prose

Figure 8-1

For example, you can be halfway between black and white, but not between man and woman. A story could be partly true and partly false, but a person could hardly be partly rich and partly poor. None of these differences matters: just because these are pairs of terms which we think of as opposites, they are said to be binary oppositions.

Binary oppositions can be neatly written down like this:

good/evil

That's the way you'll find them written in this chapter.

What kinds of things can be opposed?
Binary oppositions don't have to contain abstract terms. They can just as well contain objects or even people. In these examples:

God	Devil
Mum	Dad
Man	God

Figure 8-2

Notice that 'God' appears twice. Just because x is the opposite of y, that doesn't stop it being the opposite of z as well. In a poem about God fighting Satan, the opposition will be God/Satan, but in a poem about Man confronting God the opposition will be Man/God.

An 'opposition' doesn't have to be an antagonistic relationship. Remember they have to have opposite meanings, or opposite elements of their meanings. So Mum/Dad is an opposition because Mum is female and Dad is male, even though they are hardly opposites like black/white, and they share some features in common (like being human parents, at least, though one would hope they have more in common than that).

Privilege

It is extremely common for the two terms in an opposition to be unequal. One will often be thought of as superior to the other in some important way. When that happens, we say that one side of the opposition has been privileged over the other.

This can happen in two ways.

1. The poem itself might privilege one term but, more often, it will simply be traditional. In the opposition good/evil, good is normally privileged.

2. In day/night, the privilege might come on either side – the night, in a poem about romance, for example, or the day in a poem about searching for the truth (because the light of day is useful when trying to find something).

You will see more examples of privilege in the next section, so don't panic if it is not clear to you just yet.

Identifying oppositions

Let's look first at some simple binary oppositions, in this short poem by W S Landor:

> I strove with none, for none was worth my strife:
> Nature I loved, and, next to Nature, Art:
> I warmed both hands before the fire of Life;
> It sinks; and I am ready to depart.

The title is 'Dying Speech of an Old Philosopher', and so 'depart' in the last line refers to death. Since we have 'Life' at the end of line 3, we can identify

life/death

as an opposition right away.

Nature/art is also present. Although the narrator loved both, the poem makes a clear distinction between the two. Art is artificial and nature is natural (none of this is surprising,

I'm sure) and that's the most likely basis for the opposition. Note that the poem privileges nature over art; you will find quite the opposite happening in some poems.

How about the first line? 'I strove with none' is ambiguous – that is, it could mean one of two things. It might mean that the narrator didn't struggle against anyone. Or it might mean that the narrator struggled alone. Either way, we can mark up

alone/social

onto our list of oppositions, which is starting to look pretty impressive. You can also add

striving/not striving
worthy/unworthy

again from the first line.

Analysing oppositions

When analysing the structure of a poem, you can use these three steps:

1. Find a core group of oppositions.

2. Identify the details which don't fit with this simple structure.

3. Work out a complete structure which accounts for all those messy details.

Finding a 'core' of oppositions

Binary oppositions tend to 'line up', which simply means that they go together. This gives you one of the most straight-forward ways to analyse them.

Look at these oppositions from the Landor poem:

Alone	Social
Not striving	Striving
Worthy	Unworthy
Philosopher	Others

Figure 8-3

The column on the left contains the privileged terms. These are the terms which apply to the narrator. When you put the oppositions together like this, it gives you part of the picture which the poem is painting.

Another result of this 'lining up' process is that you might easily find additional oppositions hiding in the poem. Look at the philosopher, sitting alone warming 'both hands before the fire', refusing to engage with the strivings of the social world. This is an opposition between leisure and work, subjects which are not mentioned by name anywhere in the poem.

Since the poem is about how the narrator has lived, one might even say that the opposition was one relating to lifestyles rather than just activities. In other words, the poem contains the opposition aristocratic/proletarian (or 'working class') in which the aristocratic lifestyle is privileged.

Sweating the details

We now have a series of binary oppositions which, we think, add up to the core of the poem's structure. But what we also have is some other, sticky oppositions which don't fit this structure – yet. Structuralism is about accounting for every little detail, and as you already know, details are usually more revealing than generalisations.

We identified nature/art as an opposition, and it is clearly an important one because it takes up a quarter of the whole poem. Yet it won't line up with our others, because the narrator loved both. We also had life/death, which apply equally to both sides of the core structure. Obviously, our

core of oppositions is not sophisticated enough to cope with
these details.

Life and death are both natural, but things are a bit more
complicated than that. The poem is about 'Life', capital 'L' –
the worthy lifestyle which the narrator identifies with leisure
and philosophical contemplation. The narrator chooses this
'Life', and although it's a love of nature it isn't natural:

Death	Life
Nature	Art
Cold	Hot

Figure 8-4

I've included the warmth of the 'fire of Life' and the cold
which comes when 'it sinks' – in other words the narrator
dies. This is a small detail, but that doesn't make it okay to
leave it out.

You will also have noticed that the 'nature' side of the
opposition is explicitly privileged in the poem, so the 'death'
side seems also to be privileged. This is extremely surprising,
but it's quite in keeping with the regret-free acceptance of
death that comes in the last line.

Pulling it all together
A structuralist analysis is looking for *the* structure of the
poem, not just 'some structures'. In 'Dying Speech – ', the
two apparently separate sets of oppositions are linked by this
one:

love/indifference.

'Do what?' I hear you cry. Well, it's another detail. The
narrator 'loved' nature and art, but considered the strivings of
the human world unworthy of attention. Normally you would
oppose 'love' to 'hate', but there is nothing in the poem to
suggest the narrator hates anything. The structure should be

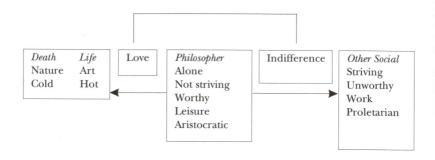

Figure 8-5

something you find in the poem, not something you impose on it from the outside.

A diagram like Fig. 8.5 would be out of place in most essays. Instead, you can use it as a map to guide you through the themes of the poem as you analyse it. This one indicates a stoical attitude, gladly embracing life and death equally and preferring contemplation to struggle. If you have been reading around (remember the advice right at the end of chapter 1?) then you might know this was related to the ancient philosophy of stoicism, and you might mention that in your essay. And your essay will be well on its way to an 'A'.

As you can see, this is a very complex poem indeed, and this structural analysis could give you a lot to say. So much for a nice simple example – but all structural analysis is like this. Because it forces you to be specific instead of vague, it helps you see the subtleties, and subtleties are always more complicated than generalities.

Post-structuralism?

The big claim which structuralism makes – to fully understand the basic structures at the heart of the things it studies – is flawed, though the reasons are rather too complicated to get into here. Once this failure became clear, a new form of literary criticism grew up in a rather peculiar way.

Instead of dismissing structuralism and starting again from

scratch, critics saw it had its strengths and that its flaws might be an extra asset. Post-structuralists typically do their structural analysis, but push it to the very limits so that it breaks down and reveals paradoxes or contradictions. Post-structuralists call these contradictions 'aporias' and some call what they do 'deconstruction'.

In 'Dying Speech – ', you might be surprised to see 'love' linked with 'death' and 'cold' as well as 'hot' and 'life'. The narrator's attitude to death is actually more like indifference than love. This would be a good place to start looking very carefully at how these terms work in the poem.

Critical techniques

Two typical techniques employed in post-structuralist criticism are:

1. Looking at the way privilege works in the oppositions. Is there some ambiguity? Does the poem try to privilege one but actually end up privileging the other? For example, is it life or death which is really privileged in 'Dying Speech – '?

2. 'Collapsing' the oppositions. Do they really stay as neatly opposed as they seem to, or does the distinction between the two terms tend to get blurred?

This isn't the place to go into post-structuralism in detail. It is a complex field of work, and the critical texts themselves are often forbiddingly difficult to understand. That shouldn't stop you from using structural analysis in a critical way. Paradoxes and contradictions in the structure can be points of interest rather than just problems to be solved. Post-structuralists sometimes approach texts this way:

(a) The structural analysis reveals what the poem is trying to say (not what the poet is trying to say).

(b) The failure of the structural analysis reveals the way language's complexities prevent the poem from saying exactly what it wants to.

Instead of this meaning the poem is a failure, though, it makes it all the more interesting. Remember, we are not making value judgements here.

Tutorial

Practice questions

1. What does 'structuralism' mean? What is 'post- structuralism'?

2. Define 'binary opposition'. Give five examples not used in this chapter.

3. What three steps might a simple structural analysis take?

4. What's an aporia? How might you find one?

Point for discussion

Are structures of binary oppositions really there in the poem? Or are they just a helpful aid to 'close reading'?

Practical assignment

Look out for binary oppositions in all kinds of things – advertisements, films, newspaper articles or any short text you come across. See if they fit into a structure which is more complex than just a single chain of associated terms.

Study tip

Read some Levi-Strauss. Don't worry about understanding it all – just get a feel for how really world-class structural analysis is done.

9

Writing an Essay on a Poem

One-minute summary – Essay-writing is itself an art form, and writing about poetry poses its own special challenges. Although examination and coursework conditions are very different, the basic ingredients of a good essay do not change. They are a single, clear idea, and a structure which explains the idea and presents evidence that it is a sensible one. A literary critic is like a barrister arguing a case in court. The issue must be clearly-defined and as simple as possible; the argument must present evidence relevant to the case in a convincing way. The particular problems associated with 'unseen' exams, 'compare and contrast' questions and writing about an individual poet each need thought, as each demands a slightly different approach. In this chapter you will learn:

▶ how to plan your essay
▶ what the most common mistakes are and how to avoid them
▶ how to add that extra 'something'

Planning your essay

The secret of a good essay is planning. Even in a timed exam, when every second is important, you should take five minutes to plan out each essay.

An essay should never feel aimless. Only the most desperate students write disjointed analyses which angle for point-scoring rather than making a coherent argument. Only the most desperate – and those who don't know any better.

Having an idea

Your essay must have at its centre one good, simple idea. Here are some examples from this book:

(a) 'The Phoenix and the Turtle' is a highly formalised, classical poem.

(b) 'England in 1819' is torn between nostalgia and hope for the future.

(c) The relationship between Man and God in 'When I Consider how my Light is Spent' is more complex than it first appears.

(d) The stoical outlook of 'Dying Speech of an Old Philosopher' collapses under the weight of its own rhetoric.

These ideas are given in order of sophistication. The first essay would simply describe the poem's features. The second finds a conflict within the poem, which is a more interesting approach. The third would explain the theme, but then put a twist in the tail: all is not as it seems. This is much better. The fourth would do the same, but with its focus squarely on the language of the text; it might even find some self-referentiality in the poem (see chapter 6) which would be better still.

Any of these ideas would be perfectly acceptable, but an idea with a twist or surprise is much better than a simple explanation. Remember that you are trying to reveal the complexities within a poem. A 'twist' doesn't disprove everything you have said before – that would be silly. It says: What we've seen up to now is okay, but really things are more complicated than that.

In a standard essay, you can't say anything too detailed and complex. What you can do is give an interesting account of the poem, and reveal that this account doesn't exhaust the poem. There is more underneath the surface, and you are a smart enough literary critic to know that. That's why a twist is so valuable to you, both in terms of honesty (you admit your interpretation isn't complete) and in terms of marks (you show you are too clever by half for these short essays you have to write).

If your analysis only gives you an explanation, ask yourself whether there is anything in the detail of the poem which might add a new level of complexity, even if it calls your initial ideas into question. Look hard enough, and you will almost always find something which will overturn your simple explanation and make for a more complicated understanding of the text.

Saying it in a sentence

These four ideas were all written in one (relatively short) sentence. This is important.

▶ *Key point* – Your essay needs a sort of slogan or catchphrase which will help keep you focussed as you write it. If your 'single idea' is actually two or three ideas, it won't do that for you. Work out an overall concept which your essay then sets out to examine.

Organising the evidence

Now you have your central idea, select only the relevant evidence. It's tempting to include any information which you think is quite clever. If it does not relate to your central idea, throw it away or change the idea.

Always go from the simple to the more complex. Start with your most straightforward information about the poem, and proceed to more advanced stuff. If your idea includes a 'twist', be sure to clearly separate in your own mind which analytical points should go *before* the twist, and which come *after*. It is perfectly fine to revisit an analysis later in the essay.

▶ *Example* – You might give a general metrical analysis, explaining that the poem is very regular, but then later re-analyse one line to show that it is an exception. That might be the very thing which creates the 'twist'.

Planning your paragraphs

Each paragraph in an essay should represent a step in your argument. Each one should take the reader a little further on. They should be quite long – much longer than the ones in this book. Go for around 200 words in each one if your essay is of an average length (1200-1500 words). If it is shorter, use shorter paragraphs. If it is longer, you would normally go for more paragraphs, not longer ones.

So, you can say quite a lot with each paragraph. Each one should be structured roughly like this:

1. one or two sentences introducing the idea for this paragraph
2. analytical evidence to support and develop the idea
3. one or two sentences to sum it up

Obviously you need not stick rigidly to this, but do be sure to give each paragraph a beginning, middle and end.

An example plan in note form

(a) Core sets of oppositions in 'Dying Speech – ' – explain the basic theme.

(b) Introduce the second theme – life/death and nature/art oppositions.

(c) Problem – how do these two themes relate? – show they do relate (line 2).

(d) Introduce the third theme – love/indifference – which explains the relationship.

(e) BUT the hot/cold opposition seems to undermine this picture.

Notice how the twist is clearly marked in the last paragraph.

Don't forget to introduce and conclude
Your whole essay will need an introduction and conclusion, too. These will be the first and last paragraphs. The introduction should clearly state your idea, although you needn't give away all your surprises there. The conclusion should sum up everything you have already said. Don't put any analytical evidence in either of these paragraphs; use them for more general material. Remember the three rules of public speaking:

1. Tell 'em what you're going to tell 'em (introduction).
2. Tell 'em (main part of the essay).
3. Tell 'em what you've told 'em (conclusion).

People – even intelligent people – can be pretty stupid sometimes, and this kind of approach will help them understand exactly what you have tried to do. If your essay confuses them, they might easily assume it's because *you're* confused.

You'll usually find these paragraphs are a bit shorter. Do avoid making them too cursory, though. Your reader needs the introduction to get an idea of what is going to happen, and the conclusion to tie everything up.

Writing your essay

Just like writing for a newspaper, or an advertisement, you need to tailor your style to your readership. Since we are talking about academic scholarship, keep it formal. The best way to learn the right kind of academic style is to read up-to-date literary criticism. There are many useful turns of phrase which you will pick up that way and which will make your writing more professional.

Who should you aim your writing at? How much do you need to explain? My advice is, make your 'imaginary reader' an intelligent fellow-student. Don't assume that your tutors know everything – they don't – but don't insult their intelligence either.

Making your case

In the introduction, say clearly what your central idea is. You can take more than a sentence over it, but if you have a 'twist' in your argument it's better not to blurt it out here. That would be rather like someone telling you the ending of a film when it's only just started. You can say something like,

'The structure of the poem, however, makes this situation considerably more complex.'

That will hopefully intrigue your reader without giving the game away.

In each paragraph, you should present evidence which you hope will convince the reader about your interpretation. Imagine that the reader is a bit sceptical and you need to try hard to make your case compelling. Try to think of objections which your reader might make so you can pre-empt them in your essay. The more you practise anticipating these kinds of criticisms, the tighter and more impressive your writing will become.

Using quotations

1. The more often you quote the poem in support of your argument, the more convincing it will be. The best essays seem to let the text speak for itself. Use quotation often and extensively.

2. Don't put words into the poet's mouth. In 'Dying words – ', the poem says 'strife', so use that word, in quotation marks, wherever possible. Don't use 'work' or 'effort' unless you have a specific point to make, because those words have slightly different meanings and the variations can be very important. Some students end up analysing a poem they have re-written without meaning to, because they haven't used enough quotes. Be careful of this.

3. In an essay on a short poem, you can account for every word in the poem. If your subject is longer you might

not be able to. Then, selective quotation becomes very important. Avoid quoting ten lines when two will do – the result could easily confuse your reader. You can assume that your reader has a copy of the poem to hand while reading your essay, so a line reference will suffice. If the poem is an obscure one of your own choosing, you could include a photocopy for your reader so that your quotations can be precise and to-the-point.

Comparing two poems

It is very common in exams to be asked to 'compare', 'contrast' or 'compare and contrast' two poems. Often these will be by the same poet or on the same subject.

Whichever of the three questions is asked, you should both compare (find things in common) *and* contrast (find differences). Here is how to weight your answer:

Question says . . .	Your essay should have . . .
'Compare'	A longer first section of comparisons, but a final paragraph or two of contrasts.
'Contrast'	A longer first section of contrasts, but a final paragraph or two of comparisons.
'Compare and Contrast	EITHER first half comparisons and second half contrasts.
	OR each paragraph finds something which seems to be shared but is actually contrasting (or vice versa).

Make sure you give equal space to both poems. Remember to have an idea and make a plan – don't just write random comparisons or contrasts. Notice how in each of these approaches, your essay gets a nice 'twist' even though the question itself just asks you to do something straightforward. This is the kind of thing which will win you marks, especially in an exam.

Writing about a poet

If you are studying a particular poet, you obviously can't write an analysis of every poem the poet wrote. At the same time, you shouldn't just write on one poem and, of course, you must avoid analysing the poet instead of the poems.

The best way to approach this problem is to write about common themes or techniques (or both and how they are related, which is better) in the poet's work by using three or four examples. Make sure there is some variety among the poems you chose unless you are writing about a specific area of the poet's work (Shakespeare's sonnets, for example).

Example

Your central idea might be something like 'Swinburne's poetry is often consumed by a dark vision of nature'. Then you would carefully pick three or four poems. Perhaps you would choose these:

(a) 'By the North Sea' – description of wild, dangerous nature, compared with God BUT result is sinister and definitely not Romantic.

(b) 'The Sundew' – about a carnivorous plant – subject is romantic love BUT the relationship with nature is paradoxical and undercuts this theme.

(c) 'Euridice' – a re-telling of a classical myth, BUT the poem becomes obsessed with a violent image of childbirth.

Give each poem two paragraphs, one for straight explanation, and one for the 'twist'. This progress – from an obvious nature poem to a poem which has similar themes but at a less obvious level – works well. You don't need to claim that the theme crops up in all of his poetry, just that it is there in some poems, and not just in the obvious ones.

Tips for essay-writing in exams

Those who succeed under exam conditions are those who stick to a few simple, common-sense rules. Here they are.

Time management

1. Divide your time equally. If you have three hours to write four essays, spend 45 minutes on each essay. Five minutes for planning leaves you 40 minutes of writing time – so after 25 minutes you should be halfway through your essay.

2. Watch the clock and be disciplined. If you are running out of time, wind up the essay and get started on the next one.

3. Write the required number of essays. It's astonishing how many students sit down to a four-question exam and turn in two excellent essays. It's virtually impossible to pass an exam that way. If you scored 70% for each essay (an extremely high mark) your mark for the exam would be 35% – a *fail*.

4. You cannot afford a ten-minute cigarette break. If you smoke, use patches or gum (if allowed) during the exam.

What to write

1. Read the question. If you don't like the way it's worded, use your introduction to twist it around to accommodate what you want to say but *don't* ignore it or misread it.

2. Examiners are looking for structured, intelligent, well-written work, not scrappy notes or random musings. Work to the same standard as you do for coursework. Five minutes' planning at the start is time very well spent – use it to structure your paragraphs in an intelligent way.

3. Examiners want to see evidence of your own original thought. They want to see something different, unusual, even surprising.

4. It has to be said that, *assuming you've followed all of the above*, the longer your essay is, the more marks you are likely to get. Examiners are looking for excuses to give you marks, but you have to say something to get a mark for it.

▶ *Don't* – let this lead you into a scatter-gun, throw-enough-and-hope-some-sticks approach

▶ *Do* – write fast and furiously.

Exam conditions

Exams are hard physical work. Eat properly before going in and don't have a hangover. Maybe you could treat yourself to an enormous fried breakfast before attending a morning exam. When your stomach's knotted up with nerves you might not fancy it, but you'll be glad of the protein after three hours' hard slog.

If you feel ill, be sure to mention it to someone in authority *before* the exam starts. If you can, get a doctor's note either beforehand or immediately afterwards.

You should be hyped enough to keep going without a break, but if you do find yourself flagging, spend two or three minutes just staring into space. It will relax your eyes and refresh your concentration, too. If you get writer's cramp, spread out your hand flat on the table, palm down and fingers apart. Rest it there for 10 to 20 seconds and the ache should subside.

There is such a thing as being too laid back in an exam. A little adrenaline will help you. If you suffer from more serious nerves, though, the best thing you can do for yourself is prepare by practising writing the kinds of essays you will be expected to produce in the exam. Give yourself a time limit; the first few you try might be a nasty shock, but it's better to get that nasty shock now than on results day. If you can honestly tell yourself that you are well-prepared for an exam, the nerves should all but evaporate.

Tutorial

Practice questions

1. What should an ideal paragraph contain (assuming it is not the introduction or the conclusion)?

2. List some sensible exam techniques, under these three headings:

   (a) time management
   (b) what to write
   (c) exam conditions

   They do not have to be the same as the ones in this chapter.

Point for discussion

Is one exam technique suitable for everyone, or do individuals work better in different ways? Discuss your own approaches to exams – both good and bad – and you will probably discover some useful new ideas.

Practical assignments

1. Reading other students' essays is an excellent way to put yourself in your tutors' shoes. You could even exchange essays with your peers on a regular basis. Most exams are not marked competitively, and so exchanging ideas can benefit everybody.

2. If you are having trouble getting motivated for an exam, do a timed essay on a short poem plucked at random from an anthology. You may get a fright.

Study tips

1. Plan essays even if you don't write them out. The plans will be useful revision aids, and the practice is good in itself.

2. If you have to sit formal exams, get hold of as many past papers as possible. Do it now, regardless of how long remains before you have to sit the exams. You may find that similar questions crop up year in, year out. Use them in your preparation, but be prepared for something different, too.

Glossary of Terms

These terms are discussed in more detail in this book. The chapter number is given at the end of each definition.

allegory An extended metaphor, usually used to explain something abstract using concrete images. (Chapter 5)

alliteration The use of several words which begin with the same sound. (Chapter 4)

allusion A trope which refers to another text which the reader is assumed to be aware of. (Chapter 6)

anapest A metrical foot consisting of two unstressed syllables followed by a stressed syllable. (Chapter 2)

anthropomorphism The portrayal of animals or objects as if they were human. (Chapter 6)

apology A poem which argues in favour of something. (Chapter 7)

aporia A paradox within a poem's structure. (Chapter 8)

apostrophe The rhetorical device of addressing a speech to an inanimate object or to an animal. Also, the device of addressing the reader directly. (Chapter 6)

assonance Sharing of vowel sounds but not consonant sounds. (Chapter 4)

ballad A narrative poem, usually in a simple form and with a straightforward content. (Chapter 7)

bathos Anticlimax, normally for comic effect. (Chapter 6)

binary opposition A pair of terms which are opposites; normally a part of a structural analysis. (Chapter 8)

blank verse Verse written in iambic pentameter without regular rhymes. (Chapter 4)

body politic A common Renaissance metaphor comparing the country to a human body, with the King at the head and the various different trades as different limbs and organs. (Chapter 5)

caesura A pause or break in the rhythm of a line. (Chapter 3)

canon In a metaphor, the part which is being described. (Chapter 5)

chiasmus A trope which repeats a phrase with the subject and object positions inverted. (Chapter 6)

collocation Being in the same place – for example, several assonances may be collocated within the same line. (Chapter 4)

complaint A mournful poem, usually about unrequited love, in which the narrator's emotions are to the fore. (Chapter 7)

conceit A metaphor which has been extended to such a degree that the mapping of figure onto canon has been partly lost or confused. (Chapter 5)

consonance Sharing of consonant sounds but not vowel sounds. (Chapter 4)

couplet A pair of lines which rhyme. (Chapter 7)

curtal sonnet An abbreviated sonnet form invented and used by G M Hopkins. (Chapter 7)

dactyl A metrical foot consisting of a stressed syllable followed by two unstressed syllables. (Chapter 2)

deconstruction The activity of seeking aporias within structural analysis, undertaken by post-structuralists.

dramatic irony A device in which a character appears who is unaware of some important fact to which the audience is privy. (Chapter 6)

elegy A poem about death, which normally focuses on the death of an individual. (Chapter 7)

elision The combination of two syllables into one by missing out one or more sounds. (Chapter 2)

enjambment Running of one sentence across two or more lines of a poem in a jarring way. (Chapter 7)

epic A long poem with a serious subject, usually mythical or religious. (Chapter 7)

epigram A very short, pithy poem, normally in the form of an heroic couplet. (Chapter 7)

epitaph A short poem designed for, or appearing to be designed for, its subject's gravestone. (Chapter 7)

euphemism The use of a softer or more acceptable word for a delicate subject. (Chapter 6)

euphuism Deliberately over-the-top poetic writing; often flowery, obscure and/or over-complicated. (Chapter 6)

extra-metrical See 'hypermetrical'.

feminine ending A line which ends with an unstressed syllable. (Chapter 2)

figure In a metaphor, the part which is descriptive. (Chapter 5)

foregrounding The use of a formal or technical element to draw attention to something. (Chapter 4)

free verse Verse written without a regular metrical structure or rhyme scheme.

foot A metrical unit consisting of two or three syllables. (Chapter 2)

genre A broad category, with a range of relatively loose conventions, into which a poem may or may not fit. (Chapter 7)

ground The part of a metaphor which the figure and canon share. (Chapter 5)

haiku A Japanese form using fourteen syllables and three lines. (Chapter 7)

half-rhyme See 'para-rhyme'.

heroic couplet A pair of rhyming lines which stand on their own, usually in iambic pentameter. (Chapter 7)

homophony Any of the many effects achieved through the use of identical sounds. (Chapter 4)

hyperbole Overstatement or exaggeration (Chapter 6)

hypermetrical Of a syllable, meaning it is additional to the metrical structure of the line. (Chapter 2)

iamb A metrical foot consisting of an unstressed syllable followed by a stressed syllable. (Chapter 2)

impressionism Style in which descriptions aim at capturing someone's experience of an object, not what the object is. (Chapter 7)

innuendo A trope which uses something apparently innocuous to refer to something much more serious and usually negative. (Chapter 6)

intentional fallacy The mistake made by any literary critic who tries to gauge what an author intended, felt or believed on the basis of her/his literary writing. (Chapter 1)

intertextuality General term for references from one text (e.g. a poem) to another. (Chapter 6)

irony Essentially a reversal of what is expected, particularly in terms of value. (Chapter 6)

leading syllable A hypermetrical syllable at the beginning of a line. (Chapter 2)

limerick A five-line poem, almost always with humorous content. (Chapter 7)

litotes A trope which transforms a positive statement into a more emphatic negative one. (Chapter 6)

lyric A poem which was originally set to music; later, any poem in a similar tradition. (Chapter 7)

masculine ending A line which ends with a stressed syllable. (Chapter 2)

meiosis The technical term for deliberate understatement. (Chapter 6)

metaphor A rhetorical trope which implicitly compares one thing with another. (Chapter 5)

metonymy A trope which uses a part or aspect of something (such as its colour) to describe the whole. (Chapter 6)

metre The rhythmic structure of a line of poetry, or of a whole poem. (Chapter 2)

mixed metaphor A trope which combines two metaphors, normally clumsily; it is generally either unintentional or humorous. (Chapter 5)

modernism A movement active between about 1890 and 1920, combining free verse with a highly intellectual content. (Chapter 7)

monosyllabic Of a word, meaning it has only one syllable. (Chapter 2)

naivety A style which is deliberately unsophisticated, aiming at simplicity of expression. (Chapter 7)

narrative allegory An allegory which tells one story by means of another, more dramatic or more easily comprehensible one. (Chapter 5)

neo-classicism A movement which saw rational form as the goal of art, and which wished to return to the model of ancient Greek and Roman poets. (Chapter 7)

octave The first eight lines of a Petrarchan sonnet, or any eight-line stanza. (Chapter 7)

ode A poem which begins with a specific, relatively everyday subject and expands it into a meditation on some more profound issue. (Chapter 7)

onomatopoeia The use of words which sound like their meanings, such as 'crash' or 'gulp'. (Chapter 4)

oxymoron A trope which uses deliberate paradox, usually in the form of a contradictory pairing of adjective and noun or adverb and verb. (Chapter 6)

para-rhyme The use of assonance and/or consonance in the place of full rhymes in a formal scheme. (Chapter 4)

parody The exaggerated and mocking imitation of another text or style of writing. (Chapter 6)

pastoral A poetic style concerned with an idealised image of simple rural living. (Chapter 7)

pathetic fallacy The use of natural elements to comment on the subject of the poem, as if they were in sympathy with events. (Chapter 6)

personification A trope which turns an abstract idea into a character, such as death becoming the Grim Reaper. Usually found as part of an allegory. (Chapter 6)

Petrarchan sonnet A sonnet broken into two distinct sections, one of eight lines and another or six; a twist in the meaning usually comes between the two.

polysyllabic Of a word, meaning it has more than one syllable. (Chapter 2)

postmodernism Style of writing which relies heavily on quotation, parody, irony and collage. (Chapter 7)

post-structuralism An extension of structuralism which focuses on the way in which the structure of the poem breaks down. (Chapter 8)

primitivism Similar to naivity, a style which borrows from the art of other, supposedly 'primitive' cultures. (Chapter 7)

privilege In a binary opposition, one of the terms will be valued more highly than the other; this is the privileged term.

pun A trope which relies on the homophony between the word which is used and a word which is not present but implied. (Chapter 6)

pyrrhic A foot containing two unstressed syllables and no stressed ones. (Chapter 3)

quatrain A four-line stanza. (Chapter 7)

quotation The direct use of words from another text, whether marked by quotation marks or not. (Chapter 6)

refrain A repeated line or stanza, common in lyric poetry. (Chapter 7)

reversion Reversal of the regular stress pattern in a foot. For example, in an iambic line, one foot might be subjected to reversion to become a trochee. (Chapter 3)

rhetoric The art of fine speaking, and especially the art of using tropes. (Chapter 6)

rhetorical question A question which the speaker goes on to answer, or to which an answer is not expected. (Chapter 6)

rhyme Two words rhyme if the portions from the vowel of the last stressed syllable to the end of the words sound identical. (Chapter 4)

rhyme scheme A regular formal arrangement of rhymes, almost always coming at the ends of lines. (Chapter 4)

Romanticism A movement particularly active between 1780 and 1830, characterised by reverence of nature and the emotions. (Chapter 7)

sestina The second section of a Petrarchan sonnet, or any six-line stanza. (Chapter 7)

Shakespearean sonnet A sonnet which falls into three quatrains followed by a couplet. (Chapter 7)

simile A rhetorical trope which explicitly compares one thing with another. (Chapter 5)

sonnet A fourteen-line poem which contains a turn – a surprising change in the meaning. (Chapter 7)

speaking picture An allegory based on a single, extended description rather than a dramatic narrative. (Chapter 5)

spondee A foot containing two stressed syllables and no unstressed ones. (Chapter 3)

stanza A section of a poem separated by a blank line above and below. (Chapter 4)

stress The level of accent or force which a syllable takes in a metrical system. (Chapter 2)

structuralism Movement in literary criticism which aimed at making a formal study of content. (Chapter 8)

style A range of loose conventions in respect of how a poem is written. (Chapter 7)

surrealism Style in which the writer attempts to imitate the activity of the subconscious. (Chapter 7)

syllable A vowel sound, often with a consonant sound at the beginning, end or both. (Chapter 2)

syllepsis The application of one verb to two nouns – one literally and one metaphorically. (Chapter 6)

symbol An image which is 'overdetermined' with many different possible meanings. (Chapter 5)

synecdoche A trope which uses a physical part to describe the whole. (Chapter 6)

trailing syllable A hypermetrical syllable at the end of a line. (Chapter 2)

transferred epithet A description which literally applies to one thing is transferred to another metaphorically, as in 'an angry letter' (the writer was angry). (Chapter 6)

trochee A metrical foot consisting of a stressed syllable followed by an unstressed syllable. (Chapter 2)

trope A rhetorical formula for making a statement in an unusual way, usually in order to heighten its impact. (Chapter 6)

underlying metre The regular metre in which a poem is written, disregarding one-off variations. (Chapter 3)

value judgement A statement which says whether something is good or bad. Academic literary critics avoid value judgements; book critics in newspapers love them.

vernacular A poetic style which uses non-standard dialect. (Chapter 7)

vorticism A strand of modernism which celebrated the new mechanical age. (Chapter 7)

Web sites for Literature Students

One-minute summary – The internet, or world wide web, is an amazingly useful resource, giving the student nearly free and almost immediate information on any topic. Ignore this vast and valuable store of materials at your peril! The following list of web sites may be helpful for you. Please note that neither the author nor the publisher is responsible for content or opinions expressed on the sites listed, which are simply intended to offer starting points for students. Also, please remember that the internet is a fast-evolving environment, and links may come and go. If you have some favourite sites you would like to see mentioned in future editions of this book, please write to Richard Cochrane c/o Studymates (address on back cover), or email him at the address shown below. You will find a free selection of useful and readymade student links for literature and other subjects at the Studymates web site. Happy surfing!

Studymates web site: http://www.studymates.co.uk
Email: richardcochrane@studymates.co.uk

Introduction

The web sites listed here are the most established or high profile ones; new ones come and go all the time. To find extra sites use one of the leading search engines like Alta Vista, Infoseek, Hotbot, Askjeeves, Yahoo!, Lycos or Excite. You can get to most of them just by typing in the name (without 'http://').

The following search terms (in quotation marks or in a "whole phrase" search) are useful:

"critical theory"
"literary theory"
"poetry analysis"

Remember that the more specific you make your search, the more useful the results will be.

There is a lot on the web for poets, and a lot about critical theory, but not so much literary criticism. That imbalance is represented by the numbers of sites listed in the different categories below.

The web sites

Basic literary criticism

These sites deal with literary criticism at the sort of level we have dealt with it in this book, or more simply. They are useful places to pick up hints and tips, but in some cases too simplistic for 'A' level or degree work.

Channel 4 Schools
http://schools.channel4.com/online–resources/

CyberEnglish
http://www.tnellen.com/cybereng/

Critical Reading: A Guide
http://www.brocku.ca/english/jlye/criticalreading.html

Exploring Literature
http://shared-visions.com/explore/literature/lithome.htm

Poetry Analysis
http://calvin.stemnet.nf.ca/~hblake/poetryan.html

Learning Resource Services
http://www.austin.cc.tx.us/lrs/litcrit.htm

Literary Criticism Page
http://home1.gte.net/turner24/critcont.htm

Studyweb
http://www.studyweb.com/lit/crit.htm

Periods or styles of poetry
There is less on specific subjects like these than you might imagine. Use the 'meta-resources' listed at the end of this index to find some in areas which interest you, or use a term such as 'Renaissance poetry' (be sure to spell it right) in any search engine. Most of the sites which follow are rather specific meta-resources.

American Literature on the Web
http://lang.nagoya-u.ac.jp/~matsuoka/AmeLit.html

Children's Literature Web Guide
http://www.ucalgary.ca/~dkbrown/index.html

Everything Postmodern
http://helios.augustana.edu/~gmb/postmodern/

Index of Modernism Web Sites
http://www.modcult.brown.edu/people/Scholes/modlist/Title.html

Literary Periods, Movements & Topics
http://staff.lib.muohio.edu/~wortmawa/litperiods.html

Modernism timeline
http://faculty.washington.edu/eckman/timeline.html

Victorian Web
http://www.stg.brown.edu/projects/hypertext/landow/victorian /vn/vicauth.html

Twentieth Century Poetry in English
http://www.lit.kobe-u.ac.jp/~hishika/20c–poet.htm

Critical theory

The contents of many of these sites are, in many cases, far more advanced than anything in this book. If you browse through them, though, you should find a few interesting ideas.

Eclat
http://ccat.sas.upenn.edu/Complit/Eclat/

Eserver
http://eserver.org/theory/

French Studies Web
http://www.nyu.edu/pages/wessfrench/index.html

Glossary of Literary and Critical Terms
http://www.english.upenn.edu/~jlynch/Terms/Temp/
index.html

Johns Hopkins Critical Theory Guide
http://www.press.jhu.edu/books/guide/

Literary and Critical Theory
http://www.stg.brown.edu/projects/hypertext/landow/
SSPCluster/

Pennsylvania University Critical Theory Guide
http://www.english.upenn.edu/~jlynch/Lit/

Postmodern Thought
http://www.cudenver.edu/~mryder/itc–data/
postmodern.html

Sarah Zupko's Cultural Studies Centre
http://www.mcs.net/~zupko/popcult.htm

Semiotics Sites
http://www.epas.utoronto.ca:8080/french/as-sa/
EngSem1.html

Society for Critical Exchange
http://www.cwru.edu/affil/sce/SCEMain.html

The Spoon Collective
http://lists.village.virginia.edu/~spoons/
Includes useful mailing list archives.

University College Irvine Critical Theory Guide
http://sun3.lib.uci.edu/indiv/scctr/online.html

E-text libraries

These are just a couple of the many online libraries containing classic and modern poetry in electronic form.

The Electronic Text Centre at Virginia University
http://etext.lib.virginia.edu/britpo.html

Project Bartleby
http://www.columbia.edu/acis/bartleby/index.html

Project Gutenberg
http://www.promo.net/pg/

General meta-resources

A 'meta-resource' contains lots of links to other sites, so you can 'surf' to useful information rather than searching for it directly. So, although these kinds of sites rarely have much other content, they're excellent places to start if you're looking for something specific.

Australian National University
http://online.anu.edu.au/english/lt.html

English and Humanities Sites
http://odin.english.udel.edu/humanities/humanities.html

Labovitz E-Zine List
http://www.meer.net/~johnl/e-zine-list/

Literary Criticism on the Web
http://www.geocities.com/Athens/Crete/9078/

Literature Links
http://www.geocities.com/Athens/Crete/9078/general.html

Menon Resources
http://redfrog.norconnect.no/~menon/resources.html

Omaha Public Schools
http://www.ops.org/lang-art/links.html
Has links about language in general.

Oxford University
http://users.ox.ac.uk/~classics/resources/theory.html

Recommended Literary Sites
http://www.empirenet.com/~rdaeley/recommended.html

Virtual Reference
http://www.comenius.com/index.html

Voice of the Shuttle
http://humanitas.ucsb.edu/shuttle/english.html

Mailing lists
There are also a number of e-mail 'discussion lists' devoted to different aspects of poetry analysis, from favourite poems to deconstruction. They are an excellent way to learn about poetry and try out your ideas. To find individual lists, check out these sites:

Liszt
http://www.liszt.com
You can search from among over 90,000 mailing lists here.

Mailbase
http://mailbase.ac.uk
This is a UK-based academic mailing list service. More than 2,000 mailing lists are available.

Yanoff

As well as the web, the internet has other, less user-friendly places where information is stored. For an overview, look for the Yanoff list (type 'Yanoff' into any search engine and a copy should turn up; it's all over the net in the form of a simple text file). Be aware, though, that lists like this are designed for people who understand how to use more arcane forms of access such as telnet, FTP and Usenet. They're not all that difficult to handle, but it's not so easy to figure them out on your own.